The endpaper maps are reproduced from a large map of North and South Carolina drawn by Henry Mouzon and originally published in 1775. The front endpapers show central and western North Carolina and the rear endpapers show the northern section of South Carolina. Many of the places Fanning mentions in the *Narrative* appear on these endpapers. The whole Mouzon map is included in W. P. Cumming's *North Carolina in Maps* (Raleigh: State Department of Archives and History, 1966).

The Narrative of Col. David Fanning

Briarpatch Press
Box 2482
Davidson, North Carolina 28036

 Tradd Street Press
38 Tradd Street
Charleston, South Carolina 29401

The
Narrative
of
Col. David Fanning

EDITED
WITH AN INTRODUCTION AND NOTES
BY
Lindley S. Butler

Briarpatch Press
DAVIDSON, NORTH CAROLINA
&
Tradd Street Press
CHARLESTON, SOUTH CAROLINA

Composed & printed by
BRIARPATCH PRESS, DAVIDSON, N. C.

For William S. Powell

Preface

SURPRISING AS IT may seem, the most important and extensive Loyalist narrative on the Revolutionary War in the Southern provinces, the journal of Colonel David Fanning, has never been published in a scholarly edition. Although the journal was published in 1861 and in 1908 with several reprints, these earlier editions were not adequately annotated, nor was the text accurately reproduced. Despite a lengthy search involving various descendants and archival agencies in Canada and the United States, it appears that the original manuscript is lost. Only slight hope remains that the journal is extant and may someday be discovered.

The text of the present edition is composed of two sections: the first being the Jonas Howe transcript, which is a partial transcription of the original manuscript and is published here for the first time; and the second being a portion reprinted from the Alfred W. Savary 1908 edition, which is the only known complete version of the journal. Together the two sections provide a complete narrative. Notwithstanding the irregularities of eighteenth and nineteenth century penmanship and grammar, in this edition every effort has been made to reproduce literally the Jonas Howe transcript and the Fanning letter in the appendix. The few additions to the text are indicated by brackets. Where possible all major places, events, and persons that are mentioned in the journal have been annotated, although not all names merely appearing in lists or as signers of letters are identified.

An editor is always indebted to numerous other scholars, archivists, and friends. I wish to express my appreciation to the staffs of the state archives of North Carolina and South Carolina, the Public Archives of Nova Scotia, the Public Archives of Canada, and the Southern Historical Collection. I have fond memories of my pilgrimage to Fanning's home in Digby, Nova Scotia, and my acquaintance there with local historian Mrs. Louise Daley and Fanning descendants Mrs. Bryson M. Denton, Lister Fanning Trask, and the J. O. Turnbull family. For making the Howe transcript available, I am grateful to the staff of the New Brunswick Museum, especially the director, David Ross, and the archivist, Mrs. Monica Robertson. Fellow Loyalist scholar Dr. Carole W. Troxler of Elon College has helped in many ways and was instrumental in securing the Howe transcript. Finally, I wish to thank my wife Lelia, who typed the Howe transcript, for her keen editorial eye, her patience, her enthusiasm, and her encouragement.

Lindley S. Butler
Wentworth, N. C.

CONTENTS

Introduction

IN DECEMBER, 1861, in Richmond, Virginia, the new capital of the Confederate States of America, appeared a slim volume entitled *The Narrative of Colonel David Fanning*. Edited by Thomas H. Wynne, the secretary of the Virginia Historical Society, and with an introduction by John Hill Wheeler, a former diplomat and a North Carolina historian, the limited edition of fifty copies was the first publication of the most significant loyalist narrative about the American Revolution in the southern provinces. [1] Although the narrative challenged the long accepted Whig view of the Revolutionary era in the Carolinas, it attracted little or no attention among the stirring events of 1861. It was reprinted in a limited edition of 200 copies by Joseph Sabin in 1865, and in 1907 became widely available to historians by the inclusion of the Wynne edition in volume XXII of Walter Clark's *The State Records of North Carolina*. A subsequent Canadian edition by Alfred W. Savary[2] in 1908 contains the only complete version of the text, but Savary like Wynne heavily edited and skimpily annotated the text. Nevertheless, in the present century professional historians have utilized the narrative in general state histories and in a few county histories.

David Fanning finished the journal of his wartime experiences on June 24, 1790, at his home on the St. John River in the province of New Brunswick, Canada. The carefully compiled narrative opens in May, 1775, in backcountry South Carolina where a twenty-year-old frontier Indian trader is faced with the awesome choice of loyalty to his king or armed rebellion and treason. The record of Fanning's formative years is sparse, but there a few glimpses of the youth in local records and in his Loyalist claim. He was born in the settlement of Birch Swamp, Amelia County,

---

[1] *The Narrative of Colonel David Fanning, (A Tory in the Revolutionary War with Great Britain;) Giving an Account of his Adventures in North Carolina, From 1775 to 1783, As Written by Himself, with an Introduction and Explanatory Notes*. Edited by Thomas H. Wynne with an introduction by John H. Wheeler (Richmond, Va.: private [Historical Documents Relating to the Old North State No. 1] 1861). The reprints of this edition are: *The Narrative of Colonel David Fanning* . . . (New York: Reprinted for Joseph Sabin [Sabin's Reprints. Second Series. No. 1] 1865); Walter Clark (ed.), *The State Records of North Carolina* (Winston and Goldsboro, N. C.: State of North Carolina, 1907), XXII, 180–239; and *The Narrative of Colonel David Fanning* . . . (Spartanburg, S. C.: The Reprint Company, 1973 [reprint of the Sabin 1865 reprint].

[2] *Col. David Fanning's Narrative of his Exploits and Adventures as a Loyalist of North Carolina in the American Revolution, supplying important ommissions in the copy published in the United States*. Edited by Alfred W. Savary (Toronto: Reprinted from *The Canadian Magazine*, 1908).

Virginia in 1755. His grandfather, Bryan Fanning, was the first of the family to settle in the county, and his father, David, had moved his family to North Carolina where he was drowned in the Deep River before his son was born. His widow remained in North Carolina with her young daughter and new son, but the struggle was apparently too much for her. She succumbed in 1764, leaving her two children, Elizabeth and David, to be bound as orphans to guardians in Johnston County (the present Wake County). In later years David Fanning would claim his father's property in Virginia, two plantations totalling 1100 acres, but he never succeeded in securing his inheritance.[3]

In July, 1764, the county court bound the nine-year-old Fanning to a guardian, Needham Bryan, Jr., a county justice, who at least fulfilled his obligation to educate the boy. Fanning was apprenticed to Thomas Leech, who may have been a loom mechanic.[4] In 1778 Fanning was reportedly working as a mechanic and loom builder in Chatham County,[5] although he said nothing of his early life other than the statement that he was "farmer bred."[6] Some insight on this period is provided by the folk traditions compiled by Eli W. Caruthers in his history published in 1854. According to Caruthers, Fanning left his guardian because of harsh treatment and fled to Orange County where he was taken in by the John O'Deniell family. It was here that he was supposedly cured of scald head or tetter worm, an offensive scalp disease that left him bald. Thereafter he wore a silk skull cap. Another tradition from Caruthers is the widespread reputation that Fanning had as a youth of being a superb horseman and a tamer of wild horses.[7]

By 1773 Fanning left North Carolina and moved to the western section of South Carolina, settling with Joseph Kellet on Raeburn's Creek, a tributary of the Reedy River in the present Laurens County. In the next two years he farmed and traded with the Catawba Indians and possibly the Cherokees, accumulating twenty horses, six head of cattle, and two slaves.[8] While guiding his pack trains over the trails of the Indian border country, Fanning acquired an intimate knowledge of the forest that would be

---

[3] Public Record Office, London: Audit Office Papers, American Loyalist Claims: David Fanning, A.O./13. Photocopy of the transcript in the Division of Archives and History, Raleigh, N. C. Will of David Fanning, March 10, 1825, Office of the Register of Probate of Digby County, Digby, N.S.

[4] Johnston County Court Minutes. Division of Archives and History, Raleigh, N. C., July 17, 1764.

[5] Manuscript Notes for a Sketch of David Fanning, Archibald Debow Murphey Papers. Southern Historical Collection. University of North Carolina Library, Chapel Hill, N. C.

[6] Wyne and Wheeler, *Fanning's Narrative*, p. xxiii.

[7] Eli W. Caruthers, *Revolutionary Incidents: And Sketches of Character Chiefly in the 'Old North State'* (Philadelphia: Hayes and Zell, 1854), pp. 144–45.

[8] Loyalist Claim (North Carolina): David Fanning.

invaluable to him as a Loyalist partisan. It was on one of these trips to the Indian region in 1775 that his trade goods were pillaged by an alleged Whig militia band, and according to Caruthers from that day a new born Loyalist "swore vengence on all whigs."[9]

At this point Fanning begins the journal of his adventures as a partisan in South Carolina, Georgia, North Carolina, and Florida. The journal is an important source for the Loyalist rising in South Carolina in 1775–76 and a minor source on the various raids of 1778 and 1779 in South Carolina and Georgia and the Loyalist activities after the British invasion of South Carolina in 1780. Fanning's journal remains the key source for the Whig-Loyalist conflict that raged in North Carolina in 1781–82. The North Carolina "Tory War," fought mainly after Lord Cornwallis abandoned the state for his futile invasion of Virginia, nearly brought the Whig government to its knees, but eventually the Loyalist ascendency served to rally the Whigs to rid the state of their tormentors. For a year the state was convulsed with an agony of blood vengeance killing and pillaging that is to this day a vivid memory in the folklore of the Cape Fear and Deep River valleys.

Who was this David Fanning who inspired such fear in his Whig enemies? Jonas Howe, who interviewed contemporaries of Fanning, described him as being "a man of fine pysique [sic], small in stature, but very muscular and in early manhood very athletic. His complexion was florid or sandy and he wore a wig. His early training made him very self-reliant, and caused him also to be exceedingly reckless and passionate."[10] In attempting to explain Fanning's extraordinary success as a partisan commander, Eli W. Caruthers wrote in his sketch of Fanning that he possessed

the astuteness of the Indian and the fleetness of an Arab, with a constitution capable of bearing almost any amount of toil; and with a patience of hunger and fatigue worthy of any cause, he might be said to be always on horseback and always in motion.[11]

Certainly after reading Fanning's journal one must conclude that if he had not been a Loyalist he would rank with the great Whig partisans—Francis Marion, Thomas Sumter, William R. Davie, and Andrew Pickens.

In July, 1775, Fanning's military service began when the Upper Saluda provincial militia regiment was mustered on the Enoree River for the purpose of receiving an association passed by the provincial congress in June. The association called for common defense against Great Britain and was intended as a test oath. When the upcountry militia rejected the

[9] Caruthers, *Revolutionary Incidents.* p. 146.
[10] Jonas Howe, "Colonel David Fanning: The Career of a Carolina Loyalist of the American Revolution" (Unpublished article, Archives of the New Brunswick Museum, St. John, N.B., 1890), p. 14.
[11] Caruthers, *Revolutionary Incidents*, p. 150.

association, the Council of Safety responded by dispatching a mission to persuade the disaffected settlers to the Revolutionary cause and by mustering the Whig militia.[12]

Although a clash was averted in September by a truce arranged primarily by William Henry Drayton at Ninety Six, the peace was shattered in November by the arrest of a prominent Loyalist Robert Cunningham, who was sent to Charleston. Cunningham's brother Patrick organized a band, which Fanning joined, that tried to free Robert Cunningham but failed. Instead they seized a load of powder that the Council of Safety was sending to the Cherokees and then participated in the siege of Ninety Six. The Loyalist victory at Ninety Six on November 22 was countered by a major invasion of the upcountry by Whig militia from both the Carolinas. This campaign ended with the capture of most of Patrick Cunningham's men at the Big Cane Brake on December 22. Fanning narrowly escaped capture and fled to the Cherokees.[13]

In less than a month Fanning was made a prisoner by Whig militia—the first of fourteen captures over the next three years. He was released and agreed to remain neutral but was swept into the Cherokee raids in July, 1776. With the Indians he was in the skirmish at Lindley's Fort on July 15 where a reinforced Whig band held the post against the Cherokee-Loyalist force.[14] The Whigs retaliated for the Cherokee raids by sending massive columns of militia from North and South Carolina to destroy Indian villages and crops. Fanning went to his old friends in North Carolina but found little haven there. Over the next nine months he was captured and released three times.

Fanning returned to his home on Raeburn's Creek in March, 1777, but was arrested immediately. After escaping the next day he attempted to reach West Florida and was captured again. Following four months' imprisonment at Ninety Six he was tried for treason and acquitted. The Loyal Militia was summoned to aid in repelling an American expedition on the

---

[12] David Ramsay, *Ramsay's History of South Carolina from Its First Settlement in 1670 to the Year 1808* (Newberry, S. C.: W. J. Duffie, 1858), I, 128–35. John Drayton, *Memoirs of the American Revolution, From Its Commencement to the Year 1776, Inclusive: As Relating to the State of South Carolina* (Charleston, S. C.: A. E. Miller, 1821), I, 126–30, 154–55, 166–67, 246, 252–55, 285–86, 312, 353. R. W. Gibbes (ed.), *Documentary History of the American Revolution: Consisting of Letters and Papers Relating to the Contest for Liberty, Chiefly in South Carolina, from originals in the Possession of the Editor, and other Sources, 1764–1776* (New York: D. Appleton & Co., 1855), pp. 123–24.

[13] Drayton, *Memoirs*, I, 324, 351, 365–71, 380, 399–403, 412–28; II, 60, 64–67, 116–22, 125, 128–33, 148–49, 151–52. Gibbes, *Documentary History*, pp. 209–10, 214–19, 242–43, 246–48. "A Journal of Col'n David Fannings transactions During the late War in America, from the year 1775—Commencing 1'st of May until the peace" (Unpublished transcript by Jonas Howe, Archives of the New Brunswick Museum, St. John, N.B. [n.d.]), pp. 1–3.

[14] "Fanning' Journal," p. 4. Drayton, *Memoirs*, II, 342.

Georgia-East Florida border early in 1778, and according to Fanning he was elected the commander of the Loyalists from his area. After raiding along the Savannah River the Loyalists were ordered to return home where they found much to their dismay that the Raeburn's Creek settlement was under Whig control.[15]

Forced to remain on the run and in the forest, Fanning was again captured in October and placed in the now familiar surroundings of the Ninety Six jail. Although put in irons and chained to the floor, he managed to escape on December 20. Three days later he was back in his cell, but by February he was again on the loose. A reward was offered for Fanning but he managed to elude his pursuers for six months. Finally, after suffering a wound and becoming desperately ill, he negotiated with the Whigs, ultimately receiving a conditional pardon from Governor John Rutledge. Fanning returned home, agreeing to accept neutrality and to guide Whig units when requested. Under these terms he served the Whig militia for a year.[16]

The British invasion of South Carolina and the fall of Charleston on May 12, 1780, rejuvenated Loyalist hopes throughout the province. William Cunningham recruited a force, which Fanning joined, that scouted for the British over the next several months. The most important action in which Fanning was involved was the Loyalist defeat at Musgrove's Mill on August 18. Following Ferguson's debacle at Kings Mountain on October 7, 1780, the South Carolina Loyalists lost the initiative, and Fanning turned again to his North Carolina friends on Deep River in Chatham County where he lived quietly for several months seeking followers in anticipation of a British invasion by Lord Cornwallis.[17]

The news that Cornwallis had cleared the state of the American army in February, 1781, and raised the royal standard at Hillsborough brought Fanning and other North Carolina Loyalists into the open. Fanning gathered a group of Loyalists to scout for the British. Emboldened by the apparent British victory at Guilford Courthouse in March, he delivered recruits and a scouting report to Cornwallis at Dixon's Mill on Cane Creek where the British rested before resuming their march to Wilmington.[18]

At Wilmington, Major James H. Craig, who had taken possession of the town on January 28, established a fortified base garrisoned with 450

[15] "Fanning's Journal," pp. 4–6. Kenneth Coleman, *The American Revolution in Georgia, 1763–1780* (Athens, Ga.: University of Georgia Press, 1958), pp. 106–7.

[16] "Fanning's Journal," pp. 6–11. Loyalist Claim (North Carolina): David Fanning.

[17] Ramsay, *History*, I, 186–87. "Fanning's Journal," pp. 11–12. J. B. O. Landrum, *Colonial and Revolutionary History of Upper South Carolina* (Spartanburg, S. C.: The Reprint Company [reprint of 1897 edition] 1959), pp. 147–56. General Cornwallis to David Fanning, McAlister's Plantation, January 8, 1781. Public Record Office, London: Cornwallis Papers. P.R.O. 30/11/84. Microfilm in Manuscripts Division, Library of Congress, Washington, D.C.

[18] "Fanning's Journal," pp. 13–15.

British regulars and Loyalists. After Cornwallis invaded Virginia in May, 1781, the British enclave became the key source of ammunition, supplies, and specie for the Loyalists in the state. Unlike Cornwallis, who had envisioned large numbers of Loyalists in provincial units supporting the regular army, Craig understood how effective properly supported irregular partisans could be in keeping the Whig civil authorities and military forces confused, scattered, and weak.[19] In that period neither side in North Carolina had a regular army at their disposal, and the domination of the Cape Fear valley by Major Craig's small garrison and his Loyalist partisans was a remarkable feat of arms.

Back on the Deep River in early May, Fanning established a strong post at Cox's Mill in Randolph County. Over the next few weeks Fanning, leading a Loyalist band varying in size from twenty to fifty men, fought a series of successful skirmishes with the Whigs. John Ramsey, a local Whig leader, wrote to Governor Thomas Burke that "from the daring Spirit of the Tories, almost all the whigs was gone to oppose Fanning . . . I do assure you Sir we are Exceedingly distressed in this Quarter what few there is of us, is Oblidge to be out Constantly or Lay in the woods."[20] The heavily outnumbered Fanning was pressed so closely by the Whigs in late June that he had to disperse his men temporarily.

When Fanning again mustered his command there was dissension in the ranks, which caused his supporters to send a petition to Craig requesting that Fanning be appointed the commanding officer of the militia. After securing his commission as colonel of the Loyal Militia in Randolph and Chatham counties, Fanning called a general muster and organized twenty-two companies. From this muster he handpicked fifty-three well-armed, well-mounted marauders to ride with him.[21] The Loyalist rising now entered a new phase directed by Fanning, who operated independently in the upper Cape Fear valley with only nominal control from Wilmington. Fanning and the other Loyalist bands so disrupted the valley that Whig militia musters could not be held, and few if any Whig recruits could be found in the region. In desperation the Whigs lashed out with intimidation, pillaging, and murder, and a wave of violence broke over the river valley.

Fanning's first blow fell on Chatham Courthouse on July 17 where a Whig court was scheduled to try and probably execute several Loyalists. Early in the morning his men surrounded the county seat, taking within two hours fifty-three prisoners, including most of the county militia officers,

---

[19] Major James H. Craig to ———, Wilmington, July 30, 1781. P.R.O. 30/11/16. Cornwallis Papers. Clark, *State Records*, XV, 423, 490; XVII, 979, 1015. William H. Hoyt (ed.), *The Papers of Archibald D. Murphey* (Raleigh, N. C.: North Carolina Historical Commission [Division of Archives and History] 1914), II, 297. John S. Watterson III, "The Ordeal of Governor Burke," *The North Carolina Historical Review*, XLVIII (April, 1971), 97.

[20] Clark, *State Records*, XV, 437.

[21] "Fanning's Journal," pp. 16–21.

RULES AND REGULATIONS

For the well-governing the Loyal Militia of the Province of *North-Carolina.*

I. NO Perſon to be admitted a Militia Man, until he takes the Oath of Allegiance to His Majeſty, which is always to be done in Preſence of the three Senior Officers of the Regiment on the Spot.

II. ... once enrolled in a Militia Company, and having taken the Oath above-mentioned ... conſidered as entitled to every Priviledge and Protection of a Britiſh Subject; and ... g detected joining the Rebels, be treated as a Deſerter and Traitor.

III. Every Militia Man is to repair, without Fail or Excuſe (except Sickneſs) at the Time ... ted, to the Place aſſigned by his Colonel or Captain, with his Arms and Accoutrements, ... not to quit his Company, on any Pretence whatever, without the Knowledge and Perſion of his Captain or Commanding Officer.

IV. The Colonel of every County has full Power to call his Regiment together, and march them where neceſſary, for His Majeſty's Service; the Captain of each Company has alſo Power to aſſemble his Company, when any ſudden Emergency renders it neceſſary, and which he is to report as ſoon after as poſſible to his Colonel.

V. Mutual Aſſiſtance is to be given on all Occaſions; but, as it is impoſſible to give poſitive Directions on this Subject, it is left to the Diſcretion of Colonels of Regiments, who muſt ... that their Reaſons for not affording Aſſiſtance, when required, are ſufficient.

VI. When the Militia of different Counties are embodied, the Senior Officer is to command. ... of Regiments are immediately to determine the preſent Rank of their Captains, in Regard is to be had to ſeniority of Commiſſions or Service.——In Caſes of Vacancies, ... els may grant temporary Commiſſions, till Recourſe can be had to the Commanding Officer King's Troops.

VII. The Men are to underſtand, that in what relates to the Service, they are bound to obey Officers, though not immediately belonging to their own Companies.

VIII. Courts-Martial may ſit by the Appointment of the Colonel or Commanding Officer, and muſt conſiſt, for the Trial of an Officer, of all the Officers of the Regiment he belongs to, except the Colonel or Commanding Officer; and for the Trial of a non-commiſſioned Officer or private Man, of 2 Captains, 2 Subalterns, and 3 private Men, the latter to belong to the ſame Company as the Perſon to be tried; the eldeſt Captain to preſide, and the Sentence of the Court to be determined by Plurality of Votes, and approved of by the Commanding Officer.

IX. No Colonel is to ſuperſede an Officer without Trial, but he may ſuſpend him till he can be tried.

X. Quitting Camp without Permiſſion, Diſobedience of Orders, Neglect of Duty, Plundering and all Irregularities and Diſorders, ſubverſive of good Order and Diſcipline, are to be puniſhed at the Diſcretion of a Court-Martial, conſtituted as above-mentioned; and by the Approbation of the Colonel or Commanding Officer, who has Power to pardon or remit any Part of a Puniſhment, but not to encreaſe or alter it.

XI. Every Man muſt take the greateſt Care of his Arms and Ammunition, and have them always ready for Service.

XII. When the Militia is not embodied, they are at all Times to be attentive to the Motions of the Rebels, and immediately to acquaint the neareſt Officer of any Thing they may diſcover, ... it to communicate it to his Colonel, or other Officers, as may be requiſite.

XIII. It is the Duty of every Perſon, profeſſing Allegiance to His Majeſty, to communicate to the Commanding Officer of the neareſt Britiſh Poſt, every Intelligence he can procure of the aſſembling or moving of any Bodies of Rebels.——Perſons employed on this Occaſion ſhall always be paid.

XIV. Colonels of Regiments may aſſemble any Number of their Men which may think neceſſary to be poſted in particular Spots of their Diſtricts; their Time of Service on theſe Occaſions is to be limited, and they are at the Expiration of it to be relieved by others. Great Care is to be taken that no Partiality is ſhewn, but that each take an equal Proportion of Duty; for which Purpoſe Alphabetical Rolls are to be kept, by which the Men are to be warned.——Every Captain is to keep an Account of the Number of Days each Man of his Company ſerves.

The ſtrict Obſervance of the above Regulations is ſtrongly recommended, as the beſt Means of giving the King's faithful Subjects, a manifeſt Superiority over the Rebel Militia, and enſure them that Succeſs their Zeal and Spirit in the Cauſe of their Country entitles them to expect.

Head-Quarters, Wilmington, 25th September, 1781.

Rules and Regulations of the North Carolina Loyal Militia. Wilmington, September 25, 1781. Courtesy of the North Carolina Collection, UNC Library.

the court officials, and three members of the General Assembly. He paroled all but fourteen of the prisoners, whom he promptly marched to Wilmington.[22] Upon his return from Wilmington on July 29, Fanning captured and paroled Colonel Philip Alston of the Chatham County militia in a three-hour action at his home on the Deep River.[23]

Shortly thereafter, a Whig attack on Fanning's base at Cox's Mill was repulsed, and he found it necessary to journey to Wilmington for ammunition and supplies. Enroute to Wilmington Fanning ravaged the river valley in conjunction with the forces of Colonel Hector McNeil of Bladen County and Colonel Archibald McDugald of Cumberland County. In Wilmington, Fanning conferred with Craig on the feasibility of capturing Governor Thomas Burke, an act that might bring the collapse of Whig resistance. Craig approved the audacious plan, and Fanning returned upriver with the much needed arms and powder.[24]

The trek back to Cox's Mill was interrupted by several Whig counter-attacks on the Loyalists. Fanning was too late to help Colonel John Slingsby's Loyalists at Elizabethtown, who were decimated by the Whigs in a surprise attack, but he received intelligence that a large Whig force commanded by Colonel Thomas Wade was shadowing Hector McNeil's encampment at McPhaul's Mill on Drowning Creek. Fanning rode quickly to McNeil's aid, arriving on September 1 in time to lead an assault that broke the superior Whig ranks. The Loyalists killed at least twenty-three Whigs, took over fifty prisoners, 250 horses, and considerable plunder.[25]

Fanning now undertook his most spectacular exploit of the war—occupation of the temporary state capital at Hillsborough and the capture of Governor Burke. Fresh from victory at McPhaul's Mill, Fanning inspired confidence among the Loyalists, who responded by mustering in great numbers. Fanning's command of 950 men was joined by Colonel McDugald with two hundred men and McNeil's seventy for a total of more than 1200 militiamen. The Loyalist column feinted toward Whig General John Butler's camp, but then turned to Hillsborough. In the early morning fog of September 12, lax sentries allowed the Loyalists to enter the town undetected. After brief but brisk skirmishing, over two hundred Whig prisoners were herded together. Fanning bagged the governor, the council, many Continental officers, and members of the General Assembly. The Loyalists released thirty-one British and Loyalist prisoners and by noon were on the road to Wilmington.[26]

[22] "Fanning's Journal," p. 23. Clark, *State Records*, XV, 557; XXII, 550–51.

[23] "Fanning's Journal," pp. 27–28. Clark, *State Records*, XXII, 557.

[24] "Fanning's Journal," pp. 29–30. Clark, *State Records*, XV, 612. Loyalist Claim (North Carolina): Archibald McDugald.

[25] "Fanning's Journal," pp. 31–32. Hoyt, *Murphey Papers*, II, 390–92. Caruthers, *Revolutionary Incidents*, pp. 171–80, 397–419.

[26] "Fanning's Journal," pp. 33–34. Clark, *State Records*, XVI, 12–13; XXII, 102. Loyalist Claim (North Carolina): Archibald McDugald.

The next morning while the straggling column of Loyalists and prisoners was preparing to cross Cane Creek at Lindley's Mill, firing commenced from a well-concealed ambush by General Butler, who had about four hundred militiamen. Carelessness of the advance guard cost Colonel McNeil his life and a hot fire poured into his Scots from a plateau overlooking the crossing. The ensuing battle, one of the largest of the war in North Carolina, lasted four hours and resulted in nearly 250 killed, wounded, and captured of the forces engaged. Fanning secured the prisoners in the rear at Spring Friends Meetinghouse, flanked the Whigs, and finally forced Butler's outnumbered but stubborn militia to retreat. Severely wounded in the left arm, Fanning was left with friends to recuperate and Colonel McDugald successfully delivered the prisoners to Wilmington.[27]

Following his recovery, Fanning returned to the fray, facing increased Whig opposition. Instead of leading to the collapse of the Whig cause, the capture of the governor had stiffened their resolve to defeat the Loyalists. The news of the surrender of Lord Cornwallis at Yorktown on October 19 was bad enough, but the evacuation of Wilmington in November was disastrous for the Loyalists, who could not hope to survive without the active support of the British. By December the Whigs closed in on Fanning, occupying his former stronghold at Cox's Mill and forcing the Loyalists to disperse.

In desperate straits the Loyalists escalated the violence in an effort to cow the Whigs; nevertheless, by January, 1782, Fanning began negotiating a truce with the Whig government through his old adversary, General Butler. Over the next five months several truces were arranged and violated by both sides, and the Whigs, sensing victory, would not come to terms with Fanning. Although the game was nearly over, in retaliation for a Whig ambush Fanning "scourged" the Whigs of Randolph County in a last savage raid in March. Colonel Andrew Balfour of the county militia and other Whig officers were assassinated, and homes were burned and looted.[28]

By now Fanning said he was trying to "settle myself being weary of the disagreeable mode of Living I had Bourne with for some Considerable time." His first step toward extricating himself from his past was to marry sixteen-year-old Sarah Carr in April. The Fannings in the following month escaped North Carolina for a truce district in South Carolina, and then arrived in Charleston in June. As the war wound down, the British evacuated Charleston, and the Fannings went with other refugees to St.

---

[27] "Fanning's Journal," p. 34. Loyalist Claim (North Carolina): David Fanning, Archibald McDugald, Archibald McKay, Algie I. Newlin, *The Battle of Lindley's Mill* (Burlington, N. C.: Alamance Historical Association, 1975), is a recent scholarly study of this battle.

[28] "Fanning's Journal," pp. 36–37, 45–46, 49–62. Clark, *State Records*, XVI, 203–5; XXIV, 489–90. Caruthers, *Revolutionary Incidents*, pp. 297–343.

David Fanning to Governor Thomas Burke, February 16, 1782. The original letter that accompanied Fanning's truce proposals. Courtesy of the Manuscripts Division, Library of Congress, Washington, D.C.

Augustine, East Florida in November, 1782. From Saint Augustine the Fannings sailed south to Matanzas Inlet, but then moved on to Mosquito Inlet at the mouth of the Halifax River.[29]

By the terms of the peace settlement in 1783, Florida was returned to Spain, and the Loyalist exiles once again found themselves without a homeland. Many Loyalists in Florida decided to join the numerous exiles in Nova Scotia, but Fanning's first choice was to journey to Fort Natchez on the Mississippi River. In March, 1784, he set sail on the perilous voyage from the Mosquito Inlet settlement accompanied by seven other families. While scouting ahead the Fannings became separated from the other exiles and sailed on to Key West where they were stopped by gales and the extortion of various fishermen from whom they sought aid. The Fannings finally reached Nassau in the Bahamas from which they embarked for New Brunswick.[30]

The Fannings arrived at St. John on September 23, 1784, and after wintering there Fanning looked over the available land on the west side of the St. John River. On May 10, 1785, he purchased two hundred acres in Kings County on an arm of the Grand Bay called the Long Reach. He farmed and maintained his residence here until after 1790, although he purchased in October, 1788, two tracts in Kemble Manor, upriver a few miles in Queens County near the present town of Hampstead. He eventually moved to the Kemble Manor farm where in addition to farming he operated a grist mill and built a saw mill.[31]

Parliament in 1783 had passed an act to reimburse Loyalists for their services and losses during the Revolution, and Fanning busied himself for several years in an effort to document his services, making trips to Halifax and corresponding with his former fellow Loyalists. He eventually submitted a claim for £1625.10s. Although he diligently pursued his claim, he shared the disappointment of many of the Loyalists, receiving a mere £36. There is evidence that later in Nova Scotia he secured an annuity of £91.5s from the government for his military service.[32] It is clear that his journal was written as part of this project to secure a claim for his property losses and military service. He completed the journal while living in Kings County, dating the preface June 24, 1790.

A friend in Kemble Manor described Fanning in this period as "chock-

[29] "Fanning's Journal," pp. 68–69, 73. Savary, *Fanning's Narrative*, p. 38.

[30] Savary, *Fanning's Narrative*, pp. 42–46.

[31] Howe, "Fanning," pp. 9–10. Queens County Registry Office, Book C, 310. Microfilm in Public Archives of New Brunswick, Fredericton, N.B. Carole Watterson Troxler, "'To git out of a Troublesome Neighborhood': David Fanning in New Brunswick," *North Carolina Historical Review*, LVI (October, 1979), 344–45, 352.

[32] Loyalist Claim (North Carolina): David Fanning. Savary, *Fanning's Narrative*, p. 40. Robert O. DeMond, *The Loyalists in North Carolina During the Revolution* (Durham, N. C.: Duke University Press, 1940), p. 252. David Fanning Petition, 1808. Land Petitions, Public Archives of Nova Scotia, Halifax, N.S.

ful of eccentricities" but "a pleasant acquaintance and obliging neighbor."
He was a member of the masonic lodges in Saint John from 1784 until 1796
and in Fredericton from 1796 until he left the province.[33] Fanning entered
public service by being elected to the Provincial Assembly from Kings
County in 1791, serving until January 27, 1801, when he had the dubious
distinction of being the first member expelled from the assembly for a
felony conviction. In July, 1800, he had been accused of assault on Sarah
London of Wickham. He was indicted, tried, and convicted of rape on
October 2 and sentenced to death the next day. Protesting his innocence
and claiming that he had been falsely convicted because of his political
sympathies and his past career, he appealed to the provincial governor for
pardon. The pardon was granted, but Fanning was exiled from the province forever and given until November 15 to leave.[34]

From St. John the Fannings sailed across the Bay of Fundy to Digby,
Nova Scotia where they found the inhabitants somewhat hostile about the
prospect of having such a notorious character live with them. Gradually,
however, he won them over, and except for a brief sojourn in Annapolis
Royal, the Fannings spent the rest of their lives near Digby. Over the next
twenty-five years Fanning engaged in farming, herring fishing, the build-
ing of fish weirs, and in shipbuilding. He accumulated several hundred
acres of land and built in the year of his death a comfortable home
overlooking Digby Gut, the entrance to Annapolis Basin. Although occa-
sionally involved in suits with his business associates, he spent his life in
Nova Scotia in relative peace.[35] He died in Digby on March 14, 1825, and
was buried in the cemetery at Holy Trinity Anglican Church. He was
survived by his wife, a daughter, Ferebee, and a son, Ross Currie Carr.
Another son David William had died in 1810.

Although Fanning had completed the journal in 1790, three decades
elapsed before North Carolinians concerned with the history of the Revolution discovered that the manuscript existed. In 1822 while preparing a
sketch of Fanning for his projected history of North Carolina, Archibald
DeBow Murphey learned through his friend Archibald McBryde, a former
congressman and state senator, that Fanning had written a journal of his
activities in the war. McBryde, a descendant of Scot Loyalists, got his

[33] Howe, "Fanning," pp. 13, 15, 26.

[34] David Fanning to the Speaker and the General Assembly of the Province of New
Brunswick, Digby, Nova Scotia, January 24, 1804. Munson Jarvis Papers, Archives of New
Brunswick Museum, St. John, N.B. Howe, "Fanning," pp. 25–26. James Hannay, *History of
New Brunswick* (St. John, N.B.: John A. Bowes, 1909), II, 274. Troxler, "Fanning," pp.
354–57.

[35] David Fanning to Munson Jaris, Digby, December 8, 1800, July 3, 1801, Munson
Jarvis Papers, Archives of New Brunswick Museum, St. John, N.B. David Fanning to
Jonathan O'Dell, Annapolis County, March 15, 1806, Public Archives of Nova Scotia,
Halifax, N.S.

information from one of Fanning's compatriots, Archibald McDugald, who had returned to the state to live peacefully.[36] Since Fanning was still living in Digby, indirect inquiries were made in an attempt to get a copy of the journal through the Reverend Roger Veits, the parish priest of Holy Trinity. Fanning, understandably suspicious of the motives of any Americans seeking his journal, replied to the Reverend Veits that "I would not Let any man have it on any pretence whatsoever, Unless I was well informed of the Use that was to be made of it."[37]

Eventually Fanning's farm and papers were inherited by his son Ross, and the journal was carefully preserved at the home. Several unsuccessful efforts to secure a copy of the manuscript were made by the president of the University of North Carolina, David L. Swain, who had founded the Historical Society of North Carolina and was collecting documentary material about the state. Finally in 1857 or 1858 Porter C. Bliss of the Massachusetts Historical Society visited Ross Fanning and was allowed to make a *verbatim* copy of the journal for publication.[38] Meanwhile John H. Wheeler was preparing a second edition of his popular *Historical Sketches of North Carolina From 1584 to 1851* (Philadelphia, 1851). With the encouragement of Swain, Wheeler made a futile trip to Saint John, New Brunswick, seeking Fanning's journal. After his return Wheeler heard about the Bliss copy now owned by Charles Deane of Cambridge, Massachusetts, and on loan to George Bancroft, the noted American historian.[39]

Bancroft supported the idea of publishing the journal and in April, 1861, the Bliss copy was forwarded to Wheeler. Wheeler was not originally granted permission to publish the Bliss copy, but the beginning of the Civil War and the entrance of North Carolina into the Confederacy apparently influenced him to go ahead with the project. By the fall Wheeler had arranged for Thomas H. Wynne of Richmond to edit the manuscript, and the notes were prepared by Wynne with extensive help by Swain.[40] The journal was now available in America, but the published version had not been prepared from the original and was incomplete, essentially containing only the North and South Carolina material. What little biographical information was included was largely incorrect and traditional. The notes were informative but sketchy and based on tradition rather than documentary research.

[36] Hoyt, *Murphey Papers*, I, 35n.; II, 389–400. Howe, "Fanning," p. 19. Wynne and Wheeler, *Fanning's Narrative*, p. xvii.

[37] Wynne and Wheeler, *Fanning's Narrative*, pp. xvii–xviii.

[38] Howe, "Fanning," p. 16. Wynne and Wheeler, *Fanning's Narrative*, pp. xvi–xvii.

[39] Howe, "Fanning," pp. 18–19.

[40] George Bancroft to John H. Wheeler, April 11, 1861; John H. Wheeler to David L. Swain, April 19, 1861; September 17, 1861; December 9, 1861. David L. Swain Papers. Southern Historical Collection, University of North Carolina Library, Chapel Hill, N. C. Wynne and Wheeler, *Fanning's Narrative*, pp. xiv, xvii.

A Journal of Coll. David Fannings Trans
actions during the Late War in America, from
the year 1775 Commenceing 1st of May untill the
Peace

Coll. Thomas Fletchall of Fairforest ordered the Different
Captains to Call musters and present two paper for the Inh.
Bitants to sign one was to see who was friends to the Ke.
and Government, and the other was to see who Would Joind.
Rebellion the first of May Capt James Lindley of Rabins
Creek sent to me as I was a Serjeant of the said Compa
to have his company warned to meet at his house 15th of said
month I did accordingly and he presenting the two papers.
There was 118 men signed in favor of the King, who declard
to Defend the same at the Risk of Lives and Property
in July 1775 — There was several advertisements set
up in Every part of the said District that there was a
Very Good Prospetearing minister to Call at the Different
Places to preach and Baptise Children

But at the time appointed instead of meeting a
Minister we all went to meet two Jews By name Filvedso
and Bapelz. and after makeing many Speeches in favor
of the Rebellion and usd. all their endeavors to delud
the people away at last presented Persecution papers
to see who would sign them they were severely Reprim
mandded by Henery Oneal and many others it Came
so high that they had much adue to Get off with their Lives the
Rebels then found that we was fully Determind to oppose them.

The first page of the Jonas Howe transcription of David Fanning's journal. Courtesy of the Archives, New Brunswick Museum, St. John, New Brunswick.

As previously stated, the Wynne edition was reprinted in 1865 and in 1907 in *The State Records of North Carolina*. The three printings made the journal widely known, but it was not until Samuel A. Ashe's *History of North Carolina*, the first volume of which was published in 1908, that a North Carolina historian used the journal extensively to document the "Tory War" of 1781–82. Ashe's account is still the best narrative on the Whig-Loyalist conflict.

For thirty years after its initial publication the journal remained in the Fanning home untouched by further historical investigation. About 1890 Jonas Howe, corresponding secretary of the New Brunswick Historical Society, visited the Fanning home, which was now owned by Ross Fanning's eldest daughter Mrs. Delmina Turnbull. He learned that the journal had been willed to another daughter, Mrs. Deborah Trask, who lived on an adjoining farm.[41] Howe made a transcription of the manuscript which is unfortunately incomplete, but it is the version nearest to the original manuscript known to exist because the original journal is apparently lost. Using his transcription and research in local records in New Brunswick, Howe prepared a sketch of Fanning, "Colonel David Fanning: The Career of a Carolina Loyalist of the American Revolution," which he delivered at a meeting of the historical society on May 27, 1890.

Howe wrote that the original manuscript "is plainly written on foolscap paper, on both sides of the sheet, and stitched together firmly, and contains 126 pages of closely but clearly written manuscript." Howe further reported that there was an inscription on the cover indicating that Fanning dictated the journal to his daughter Ferebee.[42] Since Ferebee was not old enough to have copied the journal in 1790, the manuscript that Howe saw is apparently a final version that could not have been done before 1800 and probably was done much later. This probably explains the grammatical and content differences between Fanning's original letter of February 26, 1782, to Governor Thomas Burke, which is included in the appendix, and the version of this letter in the Howe transcription.

When Howe described the expression of the original journal he said that the "language is very plain, and the mode of expression quaint, and the 'transactions' briefly and tersely related; the spelling, however, is often very defective."[43] Howe's transcription appears to be a careful *verbatim* copy which shows a sensitivity to the original language that is not evident in the Bliss copy nor in the work of the previous editors. Until the original journal is found, which is unlikely considering the extensive search that has been made in both Canada and the United States, the Howe transcript is the closest to the original journal available today. For this reason, therefore, it is the basis of the present edition.

[41] Howe, "Fanning," p. 16.
[42] Howe, "Fanning," p. 2.
[43] Howe, "Fanning," p. 2.

The other edition of Fanning's journal was edited in 1908 by a county judge and local historian, Alfred W. Savary. Like Howe, he worked with the original manuscript, and for the first time the complete journal, including Fanning's travails in Florida, was published in *The Canadian Magazine* and in a reprint edition of 125 copies. Savary found the manuscript with "little or no punctuation, and the orthography and too free use of initial capitals is perhaps a little more irregular than was common in those days."[44] He admitted modernizing the punctuation and capitalization and correcting verb tenses,[45] but the flavor of Fanning's "quaint" eighteenth century expression was lost under the well-intentioned but heavy-handed editing of Savary. The Savary edition, however, has been valuable because it has been the only complete publication of the journal; consequently, the last portion of the journal from Savary is included in this edition.

Now after the passage of nearly two centuries, David Fanning can speak for himself in his own words. The residue of bitterness left by the excesses of the Whig-Loyalist conflict that embroiled the Carolinas has mellowed with time; yet, the Loyalists have borne the guilt for this violent upheaval too long. American historians, especially in the earlier generations, conveniently ignored such observations as the one made by the Whig General Stephen Drayton, who wrote from Cross Creek in July, 1781, that

I believe firmly, that we have by our own imprudencies & irregular proceedings made more Enemies, than have become so from mere inclination; . . . Civil Wars are always attended with something horrid. The bare idea of Friend against Friend & nearest Relatives in armed opposition shocks human nature! But good God! Sir, let us not countenance barbarities that would disgrace the savage![46]

A master of partisan warfare, David Fanning was truly, in the words of an earlier biographer, "one of the most extraordinary men evolved by the Revolutionary War."[47] The herculean effort of the daring and resourceful Fanning in 1781 produced temporary victories in North Carolina, but the depth and size of the Whig commitment was clearly underestimated by the Loyalists. Nevertheless, if the British had been able to adjust their Southern strategy and properly support the success of Craig and Fanning in the Cape Fear valley, the outcome in North Carolina might have been different. Regrettably for the Loyalists, Lord Cornwallis had turned his back on the state five months before the climax of Fanning's campaign at Hillsborough. With the Yorktown surrender only a month away, there was no chance for the British to assess this backwater operation.

[44] Savary, *Fanning's Narrative*, 5.

[45] Alfred W. Savary to Stephen B. Weeks, Anapolis Royal, October 12, 1908. North Carolina Collection, University of North Carolina Library, Chapel Hill, N. C.

[46] Clark, *State Records*, XV, 511.

[47] Samuel A'Court Ashe *et al.* (eds.), *Biographical History of North Carolina From Colonial Times to the Present* (Greensboro, N. C.: Charles L. Van Noppen, 1905–17), V, 90.

What was left for the Loyalist exiles who risked their lives and fortunes in defense of the Crown? In the words of David Fanning they were

striped of their property, Drove from their homes, deprived of their wives and children, Robbed of a free and mild Government, betrayed and deserted by their friends, what can Repay them for their misery. Dragged out a wretched life of obscurity and want, heaven only which Smoothe the Rugged paths can Reconcile them to misfortunes.[48]

[48] "Fanning's Journal," p. 22.

A Journal of Col^n. David Fannings transactions During the late War in America, from the year 1775—Commencing 1^ts of May until the peace

Col^n Thomas Fleachall[1] of Fairforest ordered the Different Captains to call musters and present two papers for the Inhabitants to sign[.] one was to see who was friends to the King and Government, and the other was to see who would Join the Rebellion[.] the first of may Capt James Lindley[2] of Rabirns Creek[3] sent to me as I was a sergeant of the said Company to have his Company warned to meet at his house 15th of said month[.][4] I did accordingly and he presenting the two papers. There was 118 men signed

---

[1] THOMAS FLETCHALL (1725-) of Fairforest in the present Union County, South Carolina was a justice of the peace, coroner, and colonel of the Upper Saluda militia regiment. He was a leading planter in the Ninety Six District with over 1600 acres and a grist mill. He was captured in December, 1775, by the Whigs and imprisoned for six months. After his release he returned home and lived quietly until after the Loyalist defeat at Kings Mountain when he fled to Charleston. When the British evacuated Charleston he went to Jamaica. In 1787 he described himself as corpulent with a weight of 280 pounds. Public Record Office, London: Audit Office Papers, American Loyalist Claims. Transcripts of the Manuscript Books and Papers of the Commission of Enquiry into the Losses and Services of the American Loyalists. New York Public Library. Thomas Fletchall, A.O./52, LVII, 223–39. Lorenzo Sabine, *Biographical Sketches of Loyalists of the American Revolution with an Historical Essay* (Port Washington, N. Y.: Kennikat Press [reissue of 1864 edition], 1966), I, 427. Gibbes, *Documentary History*, I, 123.

[2] JAMES LINDLEY (1735-1779), a native of Chester County, Pa., lived in Orange County, N. C., and settled on Reaburn's Creek by 1768 in the area that became the Ninety Six District. He was justice of the peace for several districts and a captain in the Upper Saluda regiment. He was at the siege of Ninety Six and was captured at the Great Cane Brake. Lyndley's Fort, the site of a skirmish on July 15, 1776, was apparently his home. He remained an active Loyalist until his capture at the battle of Kettle Creek in Georgia on February 14, 1779. Imprisoned in the Ninety Six jail, he was tried, convicted, and hanged in April, 1779. Gibbes, *Documentary History*, I, 25–26, 250. *South Carolina Gazette*, Charleston, S. C., February 2, 1769; January 23, 1775. Claim of William Moore, sheriff of Ninety Six District, Revolutionary Records, Audited Accounts #5335. South Carolina Department of Archives and History, Columbia, S. C. Colonial Land Plats, South Carolina Department of Archives and History, Columbia, S. C., XV, 248; XVI, 315.

[3] Raeburn's Creek is a tributary of Reedy River and is located in the present Laurens County, South Carolina. The name was variously spelled as Raebern's, Rayborn's, Raborn's, and Reaburn's.

[4] The phrase "15th of said month" refers to July rather than May. The Provincial Association, which was used as a test oath, was approved by the Second Provincial Congress

in favor of the King, who Declard To Defend the same at the Risk of Lives and Property in July 1775—there was several advertisements set up in Every part of the said District that there was a Very Good prispetearing minister to call at the Different Places to preach and Baptise Children.[5]

But at the time appointed instead of meeting a Minister we all went to meet two Jews By name Silvedsor[6] and Rapely,[7] and after makeing many Speeches in favor of the Rebellion and us^d all their endeavors to Delude the people away at last presented Revelution papers to see who would sign them[.] they were severely Reprimamanded by Henery Oneal[8] and many others[.] it Came so high that they had much adue to Get off with their Lives. the Rebels then found that we was fully Determind to oppose them. They Began to embody in the last of said month to Compell all to join them or to take away our arms: Our Officers Got word of their Intentions; I then Got orders From the Capt to warn the militia to assemble themselves, at Hugh

which met in June. At the bidding of the Council of Safety, Colonel Fletchall called a regimental muster which was held on July 13. Drayton, *Memoirs*, I, 155, 246, 252, 255, 285–86, 312. Gibbes, *Documentary History*, I, 123.

[5] The minister referred to here was probably WILLIAM TENNENT, who with WILLIAM HENRY DRAYTON had been appointed by the Council of Safety on July 23, 1775, to convince the upcountry of the rightness of the Whig cause. William Tennent (1740-1777) was born in New Jersey and educated at Princeton. He had come to Charleston in 1772 as minister of the Independent Church. William Henry Drayton (1742-1779), as president of the Provincial Congress, was a key figure in the Revolutionary movement in South Carolina. He was appointed chief justice of the state in 1776 and later he served in the Continental Congress. Ramsay, *History*, II, 252, 274–75. Drayton, *Memoirs, passim*. Gibbes, *Documentary History*, I, 105–6.

[6] FRANCIS SALVADOR was born in England, arrived in South Carolina in 1773, and settled in the Ninety Six District. He was a member of the Provincial Congress in January, 1775, and the General Assembly. While serving as a volunteer with Major Andrew Williamson's force during the Indian uprising of 1776, he was killed in an ambush at Essenecca on the Keowee River on August 1, 1776. Drayton, *Memoirs*, II, 340–41, 345–48, 363–65, 370.

[7] RICHARD ANDREWS RAPLEY was a leading planter of the Ninety Six District and a close friend of Salvador. He was a member of the General Assembly and the Provincial Congress of 1775 and the General Assembly in 1776. He furnished extensive supplies and provisions for the revolutionary forces throughout the war. Drayton, *Memoirs*, II, 348. Audited Accounts #6249. William Edwin Hemphill and Wylma Anne Wates (eds.), *The State Records of South Carolina: Extracts from the Journals of the Provincial Congresses, 1775-1776* (Columbia, S. C.: South Carolina Archives, 1960), pp. 6, 24, 76. William Edwin Hemphill, Wylma Anne Wates, and R. Nicholas Olsberg (eds.), *The State Records of South Carolina: Journals of the General Assembly and the House of Representatives, 1776-1780* (Columbia, S. C.: University of South Carolina Press, 1970), p. 306.

[8] HENRY O'NEAL was an early Loyalist leader who was with Patrick Cunningham when the Cherokee powder was seized. An order was issued for his arrest and he was in custody by February, 1776. With other Loyalist leaders he was excluded from pardon on April 11, 1776, by the General Assembly. Hemphill and Wates, *Provincial Congresses*, pp. 101, 104, 106, 176. Hemphill, Wates, Olsberg, *General Assembly*, p. 51.

Oneals mill which was done by Several Captains Companys and Continued for Several Days under arms, And then both parties was Determind on this Condicition That neither parties should intercept Each other[.] this Continued for Some time untill the Rebels had taken Thomas Brown[9] who after that had the Honor to be Col[n] of the Rigement of the East Florida Rangers at Augusta and Burnt his feet tard featherd and cut off His hair, and after that he got so that he was able to Set on horse Back. he came to our poast and the Rebels then began to embody again. Col[n] Fletchall formd a large Camp and marchd from the Liberty Springs to Mill Creek on our way twords Ninety Six. 12 miles from Ninety Six the Rebels found that they was not Strong Enough for us Sent an Express to Col[n] Fletchall—to come and treat with them which Said Fletchall Did but the terms of their treatment I Dont Know[.] we Was all Dismist untill further Orders[.][10] in a Short time After the Rebels took Capt. Robert Cunningham[11] and Carried him of to Charlstown[.] our party[12] was then Informd of his being taken off in the night time and by making an Enquiery after him we got Information of a large

[9] THOMAS BROWN settled on the Broad River in Georgia in 1773. Following his participation in the South Carolina Loyalist rising he fled to St. Augustine where he was commissioned lieutenant colonel of the Carolina King's Rangers (June 1, 1776). The rangers conducted numerous border raids and were in the expedition that took Savannah in 1779. Brown was then appointed to command British and Loyalist forces in upper Georgia. He was captured at Augusta in June, 1781, was exchanged, and served until the end of the war in Florida. He had been appointed superintendent of the Creek and Cherokee nations in 1778. After the war he settled in Nassau in the Bahamas and died on St. Vincent in 1825. Wilbur Henry Siebert (ed.), *Loyalists in East Florida 1774 to 1785; The Most Important Documents Pertaining Thereto Edited With An Accompanying Narrative* (Deland, Fla.: Florida State Historical Society, 1929), II, 323–25. Gary Olson, "Loyalists and the American Revolution: Thomas Brown and the South Carolina Backcountry, 1775–1776," *South Carolina Historical Magazine*, LXVIII (October, 1967), *passim*. Sabine, *Loyalist Sketches*, I, 260–65. Coleman, *Revolution in Georgia*, pp. 65–66, 127, 131–34.

[10] The Treaty of Ninety Six, September 16, 1775, was negotiated by Thomas Fletchall and William Henry Drayton. By the terms of the treaty both parties agreed to disband their forces and maintain neutrality. The treaty effectively defused the Loyalist rising. Gibbes, *Documentary History*, I, 184–86. Drayton, *Memoirs*, I, 399–403.

[11] ROBERT CUNNINGHAM, a native of Pennsylvania, settled in the area that became Ninety Six District by 1766. With his brother Patrick, he was an active Loyalist and advised Colonel Fletchall against any negotiations with the Whigs. Robert Cunningham refused to abide by the Treaty of Ninety Six and on October 23 he was arrested by the Whigs and jailed in Charleston. He was released after a year and lived in Charleston until the British captured the city in 1780. Cunningham was commissioned brigadier general of the provincial militia on November 22 and established a post in the Ninety Six District. At the end of the war, Cunningham went first to St. Augustine, then to Nova Scotia, and finally in 1786, to Nassau in the Bahamas where he died in 1813. Siebert, *Loyalists in East Florida*, II, 315–16. Sabine, *Loyalist Sketches*, I, 346–47. Colonial Land Plats, VIII, 527; X, 198; XIV, 287. Loyalist Claim (South Carolina): Robert Cunningham, LIV, 317–25.

[12] PATRICK CUNNINGHAM commanded the Loyalist force that attempted to rescue Robert Cunningham and then seized the Indian ammunition. After just six weeks of relative

Quantity of Ammonition that was there, on Its way to the Cherichee Nation for Cap[t] Richard Pares[13] to Bring the Indians Down into the Settlement where The friends of Goverment Livd to murder all they Could. We Intercepted the Amonition and took Cap[t] R. Pares who Swore to those facts.[14] we then formd a Large Camp and Col[n] Fletchall Being So Heavy he gave up the Command to Maj[r] Joseph Robenson.[15]

In the month of November 1775 the South Carolina Militia of which I was at that time Sergeant Under the Command of Major Joseph Robinson laid Seige to a Fort erected by the Rebels at Ninety Six Commaned by Col[n]

peace these incidents provoked the second Loyalist rising. Patrick Cunningham settled in Ninety Six before 1769 and became a deputy surveyor of the province. Following the Loyalist failure in December, 1775, Cunningham was captured in February, 1776. He was soon released and remained in Charleston until the British captured the city in 1780. He was commissioned a militia colonel. After the war he stayed in East Florida two years, but in 1785 he returned to South Carolina, was restored to his political rights, and eventually was elected to the legislature. He died in 1794. Siebert, *Loyalists in East Florida*, II, 315–16. Sabine, *Loyalist Sketches*, I, 347. Colonial Land Plats, XI, 37, 276.

[13] RICHARD PEARIS, originally from Ireland, moved to Ninety Six District in 1768 from Virginia. He had thousands of acres of land in backcountry South Carolina with plantations on the Reedy and Saluda rivers, and later the Enoree River. He filed a claim for over £15,000 in losses including land, a grist mill, a saw mill, a number of slaves, an Indian store, and large numbers of livestock. In Virginia he served in the provincial forces in the French and Indian War and as an Indian agent. After defecting to the Loyalists in South Carolina he was arrested and held nine months while his plantations were destroyed by the Whig militia and his family driven from home. Following his release by the Whigs he went to Pensacola in West Florida and was commissioned a provincial captain. After the British invasion of South Carolina he was ordered by Clinton to pacify the backcountry and served as an acting lieutenant colonel of the militia. When the British evacuated South Carolina he went to East Florida and finally to Abaco in the Bahamas. Loyalist Claim (South Carolina): Richard Pearis, XXVI, 362–85. Carole Watterson Troxler, "The Migration of Carolina and Georgia Loyalists to Nova Scotia and New Brunswick" (unpublished Ph.D. dissertation, University of North Carolina, Chapel Hill, N. C., 1974), p. 296. Hemphill, Wates, Olsberg, *General Assembly*, pp. 62–63.

[14] The powder and lead seized by Patrick Cunningham's Loyalists on November 3, 1775, had been granted to the Cherokees as a treaty gift by the Council of Safety. Captain Richard Pearis, in command of the Whig guard, defected and gave credence to the rumor that the powder was being supplied to the Cherokees by the Whigs on the the condition that they attack the Loyalist frontier settlers. William Drayton ordered the militia to "apprehend the King's mad people concerned in this daring act." Drayton, *Memoirs*, I, 407–8; II, 64, 116. Hemphill and Wates, *Provincial Congresses*, p. 107.

[15] JOSEPH ROBINSON had 400 acres on the Broad River, was a deputy surveyor, and was a major in the Upper Saluda militia regiment. Following his successful siege of Ninety Six, he was captured at the Great Cane Brake on December 22, 1775. He was released and went to Pensacola and then St. Augustine where he was commissioned lieutenant colonel of the South Carolina Royalists in 1778. After the Evacuation of Charleston he was in East Florida, Jamaica, and finally New Brunswick. Sometime after 1788 he moved to Prince Edward Island. Siebert, *Loyalists in East Florida*, I, 52. Troxler, "Migration of Loyalists," p. 329. Loyalist Claim (South Carolina): Joseph Robinson, A.O./49, XXVI, 402–19.

Mason[16] which continued for the space of three Days and Three nights at the Expiration of which time the Rebels were forst to Surrender, and give up the Fort and Artillery[17]

Major Robinson then Ordered the militia to the North Side of Saluda River and Discharg[d] them for Eighteen Days[.] afterwards Orders was Issued for every Cap[t] to Collect their Respective Companies at Hendricks mill about 20 miles from Ninety Six[.] the Rebels having Receivd Inteligence of our Intended motions they Immediately marched before us and took possession of the Grounds which prevented our assembling there.

But about 300 of our men met at Little River and marched from thence to Reedy River and Encamped at the big Cane Break for Several Days—the Rebels being informed of our Situation march[d] unexpectedly upon us and made prisoners of 130 of our men[.][18] the Remainder fled into the woods and continued there—with the Cherichee Indians untill the 18th of January 1776—when I was made prisoner by a party of Rebels commaned by a Captain John Burns,[19] who after Detaining me four days and Repeatedly urging me to take the Oath of Allegiance to the United States Stript me of Every thing and made me give Security for my future good Behaviour by which means I got clear on the 10 of may 1776. hearing the Rebels had Issued a Proclamation to all the friends of Goverment offering them pardon and protection provided they would Return to their Respective habitations & Remain neutral this Indused for to Return to my home where

---

[16] JAMES MAYSON, a justice of the peace of the Ninety Six District, held commissions in 1775 as lieutenant colonel of the Ninety Six militia regiment and as major in the provincial rangers. He was a member from his district in the provincial congresses of 1775. He was a member of the General Assembly of 1776 and in the period 1778–80. Although Mayson held a colonel's rank in the militia, Major Andrew Williamson was actually considered the commander at Ninety Six. Apparently they exercised a joint command in practice. Hemphill and Wates, *Provincial Congresses*, pp. 6, 24, 45, 76. Hemphill, Wates, Olsberg, *General Assembly*, pp. 14, 306, 322. Edward McCrady, *The History of South Carolina in the Revolution, 1775–1780* (New York: MacMillan Co., 1901), pp. 11–12.

[17] The siege of Ninety Six, November 19–22, 1775, was a Loyalist victory. The Whig militia had gathered at Ninety Six under the command of Major Andrew Williamson and Major James Mayson. McCrady, *South Carolina in the Revolution*, p. 90. Drayton, *Memoirs*, II, 116–23, 148–52.

[18] The battle of the Great Cane Brake on December 22, 1775, was a brief skirmish that ended the second Loyalist rising. The Whig militia commanded by Colonel Richard Richardson and Lieutenant Colonel William Thomson were reinforced by North Carolina militia under Colonel William Polk and Lieutenant Colonel Alexander Martin. Colonel Thomson led the force that surprised the Loyalists and captured the bulk of them. On December 23 a huge snowfall began and the campaign was thereafter dubbed the "Snow Campaign." Drayton, *Memoirs*, II, 124–32. Gibbes, *Documentary History*, I, 242–43, 246–48.

[19] JOHN BURNS cannot be positively identified, although at least two men of this name were in military service in South Carolina.

I arriv^d on the 15th of June. on the 20th the Rebels Being apprehensive of the Cherichee Indians breaking out dispatched several of their Emissaries amongst the Loyalists for to Discover their Intentions. one of which was Capt Ritche,[20] who came to me and told me that he was a friend to Goverment and some time before—left the Indian Nation and then wanted a Pilot to conduct him to the Indian nation again—I agreed to Conduct him to any part of the Country he wanted for to go provided he would Keep it secret. this he promised for to do But Immediately went and lodg^d an Information against me and swore that I then had a Company of men Ready in order for to Join the Indians[.] in Consequence of this I was made prisoner again—on the 25th by a Capt. John Rogers,[21] and thrown into close confinement with three Centinels over me. On the 1st of July the Indians came down into the Back Country of South Carolina and Kild Several families—at which time the Rebel Camp being in Great Confusion I made my Escape and went to my own house at Rabirns Creek but finding a number of my friends had already Gone to the Indians and more Dispos^d so for to do. I Got 25 men for to join me and on our arrival at Pareshers plantation[22] on Reedy River in the Indian land we formed a Junction with the Indians[.] on the 15th in the Evening the militia and the Cherichees to the amount of 260 Sarrounded a fort Built with Loggs containing 450 of the Rebels and after a smart fire on both sides for two hours and a half we Retreated without—any Injury Except one of the Indian Chiefs being Shot through the hand.[23] I then left

[20] Probably the WILLIAM RITCHIE, a militia captain, who persecuted the family of William Cunningham (later called "Bloody Bill"). Ritchie killed John Cunningham who was lame, mistreated the father, and threatened the life of William Cunningham who had fled to Savannah. Cunningham returned to Ninety Six and killed Ritchie. The brothers Robert and Patrick Cunningham were cousins of William Cunningham (see footnote 39). Siebert, *Loyalists in East Florida*, II, 314. A. S. Salley, Jr. (ed.), *Stub Entries to Indents Issued in Payment of Claims Against South Carolina Growing out of the Revolution* (Columbia, S. C.: Historical Commission of South Carolina, 1925), X, part 2, 47.

[21] JOHN ROGERS received land grants in Craven County in 1771. He served in the provincial congress in 1775 as a delegate from the upper district between the Broad and Saluda rivers. The next year he represented his district in the General Assembly and was a justice of the peace for the Ninety Six District. He was present at the siege of Ninety Six as a captain of militia. Colonial Land Plats, XX, 176, 188, 191, 193; XXIV, 69, 502. Hemphill and Wates, *Provincial Congresses*, p. 78. Hemphill, Wates, Olsberg, *General Assembly*, pp. 14, 306. Drayton, *Memoirs*, II, 150.

[22] This rendezvous was the plantation of Richard Pearis, who had a vast estate that he had secured from the Cherokees through his natural son. Loyalist Claim (South Carlina): Richard Pearis, XXVI, 362–405.

[23] Lyndley's Fort was located on Reaburn's Creek in present Laurens County and was presumably the home of James Lindley. The skirmish was fought on July 15, 1776, and the Whig victory was the turning point in the Indian uprising in South Carolina. Militia from North and South Carolina later ravaged the Cherokee mountain towns in a major campaign. Whig sources claim at least two Indians were killed. McCrady, *South Carolina in the*

the Indians and pursued my way to North Carolina, where on my arrival I was taken up again and Close Confin^d but was rescued by my friends three Different times after which I made my Escape Good. I then Endeavor^d for to go home again, and after Experiencing a numberless hardships in the woods I arrived the 10th of March 1777 at Rebuns Creek South Carolina—I was made prisoner again on the 11th by a Capt Smith bound—hand and foot and carried under Guard towards Ninety Six Goal after marching 12 miles the Company halted for the evning and I watching an opportunity I cut the Ropes I was bound with and Stript myself[.] when the Guard was asleep I threw myself out of the window and Returned back to Reburns Creek by a Different way from that which they had—Carried me prisoner. I was obliged now for to seret myself in the woods until August and was supplied with provition by some Quakers and other Loyalists in the neighbourhood.—

A Company of Loyalists of which—I was one, was thin Raised by a Richard Parish[24] and it was determined to Go to mobile and Join the British army but one of the Company proving treacherous Gave information to the Rebels who Raised a body of Troops. for to Supress us[.] they took me with five more prisoners and Carried us to Ninety Six Goal[.] the 5th of August 1777 Captain Parish escaped with some of the Loyalists Belonging to the Company and made his way Good to the British army at mobile in West Floriday—Myself with the five others who where taken Remain^d in Close Confinement untill november following and were then tried for our Lives on a Charge of high Treason for Rising in arms against the United States of America but where Acquited and went home[.] the fees and expences of my Confinement amounted to 300 £ Virgina money allowing Dollars at 6 Shillings each which I paid and was then Ordered back to the Goal for the Rent of the Room.

the 1st of march 1778. Capt. John York of East Florida. Received Orders from the Commander in Chief for the Loyal militia of Georgia and South Carolina to assemble themselves accordingly they were embodied. the majority of the people chose me their Commaning Officer[.] we took a number of prisoners furnished ourselves with horses and marched to Savannah River on the Borders of Georgia 12 miles above Augusta.[25] Capt

---

Revolution, pp. 192–94. Drayton, *Memoirs*, II, 342, 365. Gibbes, *Documentary History*, II, 24–26, 30–31.

[24] RICHARD PEARIS, see footnote 13. Pearis states that he raised a force of 400 to go to West Florida. Loyalist Claim (South Carolina): Richard Pearis, XXVI, 376.

[25] These border raids by the South Carolina and Georgia militia were apparently designed to disrupt the impending Whig invasion of Florida under Major General Robert Howe. The poorly organized and supplied invasion was aborted at the border in July. Coleman, *Revolution in Georgia*, pp. 106–8.

York who was our Pilot then Got discouraged and would not Suffer any of the militia to proceed with him back to East Florida except three men; we were then under the necessity of Returning home upwards of 100 miles through the Rebels Country and betake ourselves to the woods as formerly. During our Retreat we were pursued by 300 of the Rebels but Got Back home to Reburns Creek safe—when the Rebels found we were Returnd they Raised a body of men for to take us and for the space of three months Kept so Constant a Look out that we were oblidged for to stay in the woods. Six weeks of which time I never saw a man except Samuel Brown[26] who was afterwards Killed at Tigo-River,[27] that shared my Sufferings and lived entirely without Either Bread or Salt upon what we Killed in the wilderness. we Determined let the Consequence be what it would to proceed to the Settlement of Green River.[28] North Carolina where we Rested ourselves at a friends house about a week, here we parted. I then proceeded to Tigo River where I arrived safe the 1st of June 1778. Myself and one Samuel Smith[29] now Associated and were Taken by a Company of Rebels Commanded by a Capt. Going,[30] we made our escape the second night by Bribing the Centinel and parted Company. I met with one of the horses belonging To the Rebels about a mile from the house I had escaped from and mounted him[.] they pursued me through the woods by the horses tracks upwards of seventy miles and Came to Reburns Creek where I lived—they were anxious for to Recover their horse from me and promised for to—Return one of four they had taken from me if I would Deliver up said horse—this being agreed upon, I went with them for to Receive my own horse back again, when we had advanced 30 miles we came near to where a Rebel fort was. I Desird them to Go a little out of the way and avoid it. which they had promised to do[.] before we proceeded on our Journey one of them laid hold of my horses Bridle and told me to surrender myself a prisoner for they were

[26] SAMUEL BROWN ("Plundering Sam Brown") from Tryon County (now Lincoln County), North Carolina, was a Loyalist militia captain. He pillaged throughout the Catawba River valley. He was assassinated by Whigs in the summer of 1780 on the Tyger River. Lyman C. Draper, *King's Mountain and Its Heroes: History of the Battle of King's Mountain, October 7th 1780, and the Events which Led to It* (Spartanburg, S. C.: The Reprint Company [reprint of 1881 edition], 1967), 134–39.

[27] The Tyger River is a tributary of the Broad River and runs through the present counties of Union and Spartanburg, South Carolina.

[28] The Green River is a tributary of the Broad River and is located in the present counties of Polk and Henderson, North Carolina.

[29] SAMUEL SMITH was recorded as a Loyalist from the Ninety Six District. Confiscated Estates: Lists of Loyalists, 1783. Return of Colonel Thomas Brandon. South Carolina Department of Archives and History, Columbia, S. C.

[30] Probably Goin or Goins, Captain GOING cannot be identified. Several men of this name submitted claims for service in the Revolution. Audited Accounts.

determined to confine me in the Fort. or Carry me to Ninety Six Goal about
80 miles off—they said that I was not in that Damn. Tory country at that
time. I therefore after some conversation concluded to Submit f ɔr to be
Disarmed at the time as they thratened Blowing a ball through me every
Instant if I did not surrender which I did and on my arrival at the Fort I was
stript of my clothes and confined close untill the morning when they tied my
legs under a horses Belly and took me Before a Magistrate to commit me to
Goal[.] however I was admited to bail for my Good Behavour and on my
Return to the people who took my horse and clothes upon asking for them I
was Retaken before another magistrate and comited to Goal under a Strong
Guard—on my proceeding towards the Goal, the Guard was particularly
Carefull about Securing me and in order for to do it the more affectually
tied me with a Rope to a stout fellow who was one of them, when I found him
asleep I took the opportunity to cut myself loose with a Knife or Reather
with a pear of hors fleames which was accidentially left lying in the Room
and throwing myself out of the window I made my escape—and took to the
mountains for Shelter. I continued there for some time when Colⁿ Mills[31] of
the Loyal Militia on Knowing where I was proposed at Several Meetings we
had to Raise a Company which we did of 500 men for the purpose of Going
to St. Augustine[.] one of the Company proved faithless and Gave Information to the Rebels who Immediately—embodied themselves and took Colonel Mills prisoner with 16 of the Company and Carried them off to
Solsbuary *Jail*. myself with 14 more pursued about 20 miles with an Inten-
tion of Rescuing them untill we were in sight of Gilbert Town[32] where the
Rebels had a guard and finding we could not effect our purpose at that time
our numbers being so small and theirs still Encreaseing we Returned
Back—the Rebels pursued us all the night and in the morning we purceived
them within Shot of us[.] we fired upon them, which they Returned, and
Continued Skirmishing with them in the woods about an hour when they
Retreated. what injury we Did them we could not tell. On our part we
Suffered no loss. here our party seperated and I made way for Holston
River[33] about 140 miles through the woods. I had proceded about 40 miles
on my way when I was met by three men, one of which Knew me, he came to

---

[31] Colonel AMBROSE MILLS (1722-1780) was born in England and settled in South
Carolina by 1755. In 1765 he moved to the Green River settlement in North Carolina. In
1776 he was with the Whig militia in the Indian campaign but by 1778 he had become a
Loyalist. He was captured at Kings Mountain and executed by the Whigs on October 14,
1780. Draper, *King's Mountain*, pp. 481–82, 510–11.

[32] Gilbert Town was the former county seat of the present Rutherford County, North
Caorlina.

[33] The Holston River is a major tributary of the Tennessee River and is located in east
Tennessee.

me with Seeming friendship and on takeing me by the hand called his companions to assist him in Secureing me, which they Did: and made me prisoner[.] they tied my hands behind my Back and feet to each other under the horses Belly and took me to ninety Six Goal again—where I was close confined for 17 Days. during my Confinement I Got acquainted with a friend to Government who Lived there by talking with him through the Grates. he furnished me with two files and a Knife by which means I cut through the Iron Bars and escaped. I returnd again to Reburns Creek and after Remaining Some time in the woods there I was advised by my friends for to make peace with Capt Gillian,[34] who Commanded a Company of Rebels on the Indian lines, as I durst not be seen by any of the Rebel party I Got one of my friends to go to him Desireing him for to meet me alone at a particular place and give him my word I would not injure him. We met accordingly and pased our words not for to Disturb or Injure each other. we continued our meetings in the woods Generally every Day or two for the Space of a month, untill we were discovered by some of his Company who threatned for to have him punnished for treating with me. however he still met me now and then and Introduced a friend of his to me who. he told me I might depend upon—one Day I observed an alteration in their Behaviours and asked them when at some distance if he meant for to Keep his word with me, he Replied by all means. We were all on horse back and I had my Rifle across my Saddle—when we were a going to part as I expected he suddenly seized my Rifle and the man who was with him laid hold of my horses Bridle[.] he presented my Rifle to my Breast and told me I was his prisoner or a Dead man. I was under the necessity to surrender and carried me again to my old Quarters at Ninety Six where we arrived the 11th of October 1778—I was stripped entirely naked thrown into Irons and Chained to the floor and Remained in that Situation untill 20th of December following, when I again made Shift for to Get my Irons off and having Sawed one of the Grates some time before—I again—escaped by means of a fellow prisoner who supplied me with some old Clothes of which I made a Rope to let myself Down[.] I Received a fall in getting Down but luckily did not hurt myself. The Goaler heard me fall and presented a musket at me out of a window. but I avoided him[.] he alarmed the Guard and they pursued me but hower I Got clear off. I found myself much hurt by a fall I got in their Chasing me. I got Back to Reburns Creek but was taken in three days and again Introduced at Ninety Six. I was Chained and Ironed as before in the Center of a Room of 30 feet Square forty five feet from the ground the Snow

---

[34] Probably ROBERT GILLAM of the Ninety Six District who was recorded as serving as a militia sergeant, captain, and major in 1779–81. Audited Accounts #2838. Colonial Land Plats, XI, 475.

beating in through the Roof with 4 Grates open day and night.—I Remained in this State Eleven Days when I Got my Chains of in the night of the 12th. the Goaler did not chain me down again, but I had still part of them. Remaining on one of my legs which weighed seven pounds and three Quarters. I continued loose in Goal until the 13th of February 1779 when I took a Barr out of the window in the night and pried one of the planks out of the floor of the Room and from thence went Down Stairs.—I found the door fast Secured but went to a breach I had formerly made in the Back of the Chimney and Got out. and one of my fellow prisoners made his escape with me also. and we Kept together for Some time after. We found a number of horses grasing in a field Belonging to a Company of Rebels under the Command of a Captain Farr,[35]—who had that night come into Town, we mounted each of us one and wrode off to Reburns Creek.—In our way we stopped at a house and furnished ourselves with a Rifle and a pair of pistols; we also supplied ourselves with Clotheing. by this time the neighborhood was alarmed and the Rebel militia Sent in pursuit of us— they laid Several ambuscades but with out effect and Continued embodied for Six months. But however I was so fortunate as for to escape, but my Companion was taken. the day after he was taken I was Riding through a piece of Timberd Woods when I Discovered a party of men, They Discovered me and pursued on full Speed for Seven miles when I was lucky enough for to Escape them but my horse falling threw me and I unfortunately lost my Rifle—an advertisement was then made public for—apprehending me and a Reward of Seventy Silver Dollars and 300 paper ones was offered as a Reward to take me. This made me Very Cautious notwithstanding which I was betrayed and fired upon by a party of Rebels in Number Sixteen.—I Received two Bullets in my Back one of which is not extracted.—I luckily Kept my Seat in the Saddle and Rode off after proceeding about 12 miles I turned my horse into the woods and Remained there eight days having no Support but herbs except three eggs, My wounds by this time being Very troublesome and offencive for the want of Dressing. I Got my horse again and moved about 12 miles to a friends house where on my arrival I made a signal which they Knew to acquaint them of my being alive, and a young Girl of fourteen years old came to me. But when she came near Enough to See me She was frighted So. at the Sight She Run off But I

[35] WILLIAM FARR (d. 1794) was settled on the Broad River by 1773. He entered the militia in 1776 in the Spartan Regiment, and by 1778 he was a captain of horsemen under Colonel Thomas Brandon. In 1780 he became a lieutenant colonel and served until 1782. In the latter part of the war he was in the brigade of General Andrew Pickens. Revolutionary War Pension and Bounty Land Warrant Application Files, National Archives Microfilm Publications, Washington, D.C. Microfilm in South Carolina Archives. Audited Accounts #2308. Colonial Land Plats, XV, 97.

pursued after her on horse Back and telling her who I was She Said She new it was me But I was Dead and that I then was a Sperit and Stunk yet. I was a long time before I could Get her to come to me I looked So much like a Rack of nothing But Skin and bones and my wounds had never been Drest and my Clothes all Bloody[.] my misery and Situation was beyond Explanation and no friend in The world that I could depend on[.] however those people Seeing me in that Distrest Situation took the Greatest Care of me and Drest my wounds.—I then got assistance and Support and my wounds dressed and taken good Care off.—My horse having been Seen by Some of the Rebel party they concluded I was not Killed and wrote Several letters which they gave one of my friends offering to treat with me and advising me to Surrender threatening at the Same time in case I did not to Banish eight families of my Friends out of South Carolina. A limited time was given for my answer but it had expired before that I Received the letters, in Consequence of which their threats were put in Execution and the peoples properties *was* taken from them, and themselves Confined. on the Receipt of my Letters the people were liberated but their properties were Still Detained.

The Second day after I treated with the Colonel of the Rebel Militia, and had an express Sent of to Govenor Rutledge[36] at Charles Town about a week after his answer Came Back with a conditional pardon that which I had done Should be forgotten and that I should live quietly and peceably at Home, and be oblidged to pilot parties through the woods as occation might Require.

Before I excepted of these conditions I advised with my friends and Company who all approved of it as it conduced both to their Ease and Safety. I Remained at home a year and twelve Days and was Repeatedly urged for to Except of a Company in the Continental Service which I always Refused.[37]—after the Reduction of Charles Town[38] myself and one William Cuningham[39] concluded for to embody a party of men which we affected.

[36] JOHN RUTLEDGE (1739-1800) was a resident of Charleston and active in the Revolutionary movement from the time of the Stamp Act opposition. He served in the Provincial Assembly and the Continental Congress. In 1776 he was elected president of South Carolina and then became governor in 1779. After the war he was on the state supreme court. Ramsay, *History*, II, 269–72.

[37] Although Fanning refused the offer of a continental commission, he admitted cooperating with the Whigs by serving as a guide for the militia and was paid for this militia duty. Loyalist Claim (North Carolina): David Fanning.

[38] The siege of Charleston commenced in March, 1780, and the city surrendered on May 12. The capitulation of over 5,000 troops was the worst defeat suffered by American forces in the Revolution and demoralized the South Carolina Whigs.

[39] WILLIAM CUNNINGHAM ("Bloody Bill"), a cousin of Robert, was a native of Virginia. He lived in the Ninety Six District by 1775 and was in the Whig militia in 1775–76. After

we Determined for to take Col^n Williams[40] of the Rebel militia prisoner and then to Join Capt Parish[41] who was to Raise a Company and assist us—Col^n Williams got notice of it and pushed off and though we got Sight of him he escaped us.

We now found ourselves growing Strong. Numbers flocking Daily to us.—I then took the Kings proclamation and Distributed them through the country for upwards of 100 miles. Capt parish had the command of the party and marched up to Ninety Six which he took possession off without firing a Shot where I found him again the day after. we marched about 12 miles to General Williamsons[42] at whitehall who commaned a fort with 14 Swivils and two companies of provincial Troops. on our approach he met

defecting to the Loyalists he was involved in a vengeance slaying of a Whig militiaman. When Charleston fell he became a major in the Loyalist militia, and in 1781–82 he led a series of vicious raids through the upcountry. Upon the evacuation of Charleston he fled to East Florida where he joined a gang of bandits led by Daniel McGirtt. He was captured by Spanish authorities in 1785 and deported to the Bahamas. The following year he was in London, and in 1787 he had returned to Charleston, S. C., where he died. Siebert, *Loyalists in East Florida*, II, 3–6, 314–15. Troxler, "Migration of Loyalists," pp. 90–91. Sabine, *Loyalist Sketches*, I, 348–49. Draper, *King's Mountain*, pp. 83n., 468.

[40] JAMES WILLIAMS (1740-1780), a native of Virginia, received land grants in Craven County by 1770. He was a member of the provincial congress of 1775 from the upper district between the Broad and Saluda rivers and represented his district in the General Assembly in the period 1776–78. In March, 1776, he was appointed a justice of the peace for Ninety Six District. He was present at the siege of Ninety Six as a militia captain and served after April 18, 1779, as colonel of the militia regiment of Ninety Six District. He saw action in the Cherokee campaign of 1776, at Stono Ferry, Savannah, Georgia, Musgrove's Mill, and was killed at Kings Mountain. Audited Accounts #8554. Colonial Land Plats. XXI, 418. 475–77. Drayton, *Memoirs*, II, 150. Hemphill and Wates, *Provincial Congresses*, pp. 24, 78. Hemphill, Wates, Olsberg, *General Assembly*, pp. 14, 285, 306, 314. Draper, *King's Mountain*, pp. 465–67, *passim*.

[41] Richard Pearis was acting as a lieutenant colonel of militia and was directing the effort to disarm and disperse the backcountry Whig forces. Loyalist Claim (South Carolina): Richard Pearis, XXVI, 371.

[42] ANDREW WILLIAMSON (d. 1787), of Whitehall in Ninety Six District, had a leading role in subduing the Loyalists in 1775. He commanded at the siege of Ninety Six and was defeated, but he was a commander of the South Carolina force in the Cherokee campaign the next year. He represented Ninety Six District in the Provincial Congresses of 1775 and was in the General Assembly from 1776 until 1780. He was a brigadier general of militia by 1779, commanding a brigade aiding Georgia and participating in the Whig defeat at Briar Creek. After his capitulation in June of 1780 he began to cooperate with the British, and according to Sabine he was known as the "Arnold of Carolina." He was captured and his estate was confiscated. William L. Saunders (ed.), *The Colonial Records of North Carolina* (Raleigh: State of North Carolina, 1886–90), X, 657–58, 340, 745–49. Clark, *State Records*, XI, 354–56; XIV, 276, 284; XV, 251. Drayton, *Memoirs*, I, 324, 353, 365–71, 399–403; II, 117–22, 125, 131, 148–49, 151–52, 338–60. Hemphill and Wates, *Provincial Congresses*, pp. 6, 24, 76. Hemphill, Wates, Olsberg, *General Assembly*, pp. 306, 314, 322. Sabine, *Loyalist Sketches*, II, 437. Confiscated Estates: Andrew Williamson #115. South Carolina Department of Archives and History, Columbia, S. C.

us within 3 miles of the fort attended by Several officers Requesting he
might discharge the Troops and Receive protection for himself and them.
we granted him what he Requested and took possion of the Fort and their
arms which they piled up. after that they moved Out of the Garrison.—
Three Days after that, Col[n] Pickins[43] with 300 men marched in and laid
down their arms.—General Robert Cuningham of the Loyal Militia now
took the command and formed a camp. we Kept scouting parties through
the country and had many skirmeshes but none of consequence.—after the
British american Troops had taken possession of ninety Six I continued
scouting on the Indian lines untill Colonel Innis[44] forwarded his march up
to Musgroves Mill on the Innoree River.[45] I then Joined them with a party of
14 men. the morning following the picketts were attacked by a party of
Rebels. Col[n] Innis ordered us to advance and Support them. which we did,
and followed them untill we arrived where the main body lay in ambush
under the command of Colonel Williams. Col[n] Innis was unfortunatly
wounded with Several other officers.[46] we engaged them for Some time
and then Retreated about a mile and a quarter where we encamped and in
the night marched off towards ninety Six under the command of Captain
Depister,[47] and the next morning I and my Small party Returned back to
the Indian lines. We continued Scouting on the lines for sometime untill I

[43] ANDREW PICKENS (1739-1817), a native of Pennsylvania, settled on Long Cane Creek
by 1765. Before the Revolution he was a justice of the peace and a militia captain. He was at
the siege of Ninety Six. By 1778 he was colonel of the militia for the Ninety Six District and
was one of the Whig leaders at the battle of Kettle Creek in 1779. After the fall of Charleston
he surrendered and was paroled. When his plantation was pillaged he left parole. Following
his distinguished service at Cowpens he was commissioned a brigadier general and
remained actively engaged during Greene's campaign in North and South Carolina. After
the war he served in the General Assembly and a term in United States Congress 1793–95.
Allen Johnson and Dumas Malone (eds.), *Dictionary of American Biography* (New York:
Charles Scribner's Sons, 1928–37), VII, 558–59.

[44] ALEXANDER INNES, a Scot, was an assistant commissary to the British agent to the
Cherokees and was living with the Indians in 1777. He was a captain in the South Carolina
Royalists in 1779 and was commissioned their colonel on January 20, 1780. After the fall of
Charleston he became the inspector general of the provincial forces in the South. Following
the British evacuation he went to Nova Scotia. Draper, *King's Mountain*, pp. 108–9n.
Troxler, "Migration of Loyalists," pp. 281–82. Sabine, *Loyalist Sketches*, I, 566.

[45] The Enoree River is a tributary of the Broad River and forms the southern
boundary of the present counties of Spartanburg and Union, South Carolina.

[46] Fanning's account of the battle of Musgrove's Mill on August 18, 1780, is essentially
verified by Whig sources. The Whigs were commanded by Colonels Elijah Clarke, Isaac
Shelby, and James Williams. The Loyalists were drawn into a concealed ambush, and Innes
was wounded at a crucial moment, causing his battle line to fall back. Ramsay, *History*, I, 202.
Draper, *King's Mountain*, pp. 103–22, 504–5.

[47] ABRAHAM DEPEYSTER (1753-1799), from New York, was a captain in the New York
Volunteers, serving in the siege of Charleston, Musgrove's Mill, and as second in command
at Kings Mountain. After the war he went to St. John, New Brunswick, and was a colonel in

met with Capt Parish of the British ameriacan South Carolina Regm^t who gave me a list of Several Soldiers that had permission for to visit their friends in the country on the Return from Florida to ninety Six. I was Desired by him for to give them notice for to Join their Regiments and on this Expedition I fell in with Major Forgessons party which was Defeated five Days afterwards.[48] The Rebels after this Begin to be numerous and troublesome and little or no Regulation amongst us. I made the best of my way to Deep River[49] in North Carolina where I Remained untill the month of February 1781.

I was During this time discovering the disposition of the people being Informed that Lord Cornwallis was marching that way, I Kept my Entintions Secret until I Received Certain accounts. I caused this advertisement to be published and used all my influence to get all the Loyalists to join me and Defend ourselves—when occation might Require.—A true Copy of which is here Set forth—

ADVERTISEMENT.

If Any of his Majestys loyal & faithfull Subjects able and willing to serve in the Royal North Carolina Regiment commaned by Lieutinant Col^n Hamilton[50] are hereby requested to Repair to his Encampment.—The Bounty allowed for each man is three Guineas and the Terms of Engagement are, that he shall Serve During the Rebellion and within the Provinces of North and South Carolina and Virginia only that During his Service he shall be Intilled to

the provincial militia and treasurer of the province. Draper, *King's Mountain*, p. 479. Sabine, *Loyalist Sketches*, I, 372–74.

[48] The battle of Kings Mountain occurred on October 7, 1780, and resulted in the death of Major Patrick Ferguson and the destruction of his Loyalist corps by frontier Whig militia.

[49] The Deep River, a major tributary of the Cape Fear River, bisects Randolph County, North Carolina. The settlement to which Fanning refers here was probably the same settlement he had visited in 1778 on Brush Creek, a tributary of the Deep River that rises in western Chatham County and runs into Randolph County. Murphey Notes.

[50] JOHN HAMILTON, a prominent Scottish merchant of Halifax, North Carolina, left the state as a Loyalist refugee in October, 1777, and emigrated to New York. He was appointed lieutenant colonel commanding the Royal North Carolina Regiment which was to be raised from Highlanders at St. Augustine. The regiment's first action was at Savannah in 1779. When Charleston surrendered, Hamilton's regiment was posted at Camden. The regiment was in the battle of Camden in 1780 and the British invasion of North Carolina, and it served in the garrison at Wilmington under Major Craig. Hamilton and part of the regiment were detached to Virginia and surrendered at Yorktown. Following the surrender, Hamilton went to St. Augustine and later to Britain. He died there in 1817. Siebert, *Loyalists in East Florida*, II, 333–35. Sabine, *Loyalist Sketches*, I, 511–12. Troxler, "Migration of Loyalists," pp. 204–5.

Cloathing pay Provisions and all other advantages of his Majesties Regular and provincial Troops, and that at the End of the Rebellion when he becomes Discharged of Course he is to receive as a Reward of his Service during the War a free Grant of Land agreeable to his Majesties Proclamation——

Of his pursuing General Green as far as Hilsborough this Struck Such a terror on the Rebels and was so pleasing to us that we Immediately disarmed the disaffected and embodied about 300 men under the Command of Col^n Pyles[.] he fell in with a party of the Rebels Col^n Lees dragoons and lost 30 men Killed beside the wounded that died afterwards.[51] at this time I was with a small party at Deep River where I took two Rebel officers prisoners and several soldiers. I then Directed my march to the place where I left Col^n Pyles and came within a little Distance of the Dragoons that had cut him up when I was informed of his misfortune by some of his party that had fled, we then seperated into small parties and took to the woods for sometime.—the day lord Corwallis defeated General Greene at Guilford[52] I was surprised by a Capt Duck[53] with a Company of Rebels where I sustained the loss of all our horses and arms, we had one man Killed on each side.—the day following myself and three more of the Company furnished ourselves with arms and pursued the Rebels who we Discovered had parted and gone to their Respective homes with their plunder.—we visited one of The houses and found 14 horses which had been taken from the friends of Government and discovering one of the said party in an out house I fired at him and wounded him in the neck with Buck shot but he escaped. we then mounted ourselves and turning the other horses into the woods we Returned back to Deep River. We Kept Concealed in the woods and Collected

---

[51] Pyle's Massacre, February 23, 1781, was a crucial setback for Loyalist recruiting in North Carolina. Lieutenant Colonel Henry Lee's cavalry and militia led by General Andrew Pickens surprised and decimated a band of Loyalists raised by DR. JOHN PYLE of Chatham County. Although Pyle had earlier signed a regulator petition, he was named a justice of the peace for Chatham County in August, 1774. At Moore's Creek Bridge he commanded a company and was captured. He escaped the following summer. He took the state loyalty oath, but when the British invaded he returned to active support of the crown as a militia colonel. In the fall of 1781 he and his son surrendered under terms granted by the state, and after he treated Whig wounded he was pardoned. Saunders, *Colonial Records*, VII, 134, 813; IX, 1027, 1169; X, 600, 631, 940, 968. Clark, *State Records*, XVI, 244; XVII, 1000. Sabine, *Loyalist Sketches*, II, 190–92.

[52] The battle of Guilford Courthouse was fought on March 15, 1781. Lord Cornwallis won a crippling tactical victory over Nathanael Greene's continentals and militia but suffered a strategic defeat.

[53] Fanning's Captain Duck was apparently JACOB DUCKWORTH, a captain of the Cumberland County Militia. Cumberland County Court Minutes, October, 1777; January, 1778; January, 1781. Division of Archives and History, Raleigh, N. C.

25 men having scouts out continually untill we proceeded to Dixon Mills[54] Cane Creek where Lord Cornwallis was then encamped. on our arrival there his lordship met us and asked me several Questions Respecting the situation of the Country and disposition of the people.—I gave him all the Information in my power and leaving the Company with his lordship I Returned Back to Deep River in order for to Conduct more men to the protection of the British arms.—Two Days following I Returned to the army at Chatham Court house after being Surprised and Dispersed by the Rebel Dragoons on my bringing in 70 Loyalists[.] I joined my company again and went with his lordship to Cross Creek and as we had lost most of our horses we Determined to Return to Deep River, and Join his Lordship when on his way to Hilsborough. General Green followed his Lordship as far as little River and then Returned to Ramseys Mills on his way to Cambden. his men marched in small parties and distressed the friends of Government through the Deep River Settlement.—I took 18 of them at different times and parroled them and after that we were not Distressed by them for some little time. after a little while nine of us had assembled at a friends house when we where surrounded by a party of 11 Rebels under the Command of a Cap[t] John Hinds[.][55] we perceived their approach and prepared for to Receive them. when they had got quite near us we run out of the doors of the house, fired upon them and Killed one of them, on which we took three of their horses and some firelocks. We then took to the woods and unfortunately had two of our little Company taken, one of which the Rebels shot in cold Blood, and the other they hanged on the spot where we had Killed the man a few Days before.—We where exasperated at this that we determined for to have satisfaction and in a few Days I collected 17 men well armed and formed an ambuscade on deep River. at Coxes Mill[56] and

[54] The British were encamped at Simon Dixon's Mill in the community of Snow Camp in the present Alamance County by March 22, 1781. Samuel A'Court Ashe, *History of North Carolina* (Greensboro, N. C.: Charles L. Van Noppen, 1908–25), I, 661. Just downstream on Cane Creek, a tributary of the Haw River, was Lindley's Mill (see footnote 98). The Cane Creek valley was largely settled by Quakers, many of whom endeavored to remain neutral.

[55] JOHN HINDS (1745-1810), the son of Joseph Hinds of Guilford and later Randolph County, was a captain of light horse under Colonel John Collier. He was a justice of the peace for Randolph County in 1779. "The Family of Joseph Hinds of Guilford and Randolph Counties," *North Randolph Historical Society Quarterly*, VI (Winter, 1972), 205–6. Randolph County Court Minutes, March 8, 1779; June, 1781; Division of Archives and History, Raleigh, N. C. Clark, *State Records*, XIV, 461.

[56] Cox's Mill is located near the junction of Mill Creek and the Deep River in Randolph County a few miles south of the town of Ramseur. It was built by WILLIAM COX (d. 1767), a Quaker from Delaware, who settled in the area about 1760. His daughter Mary married James Lindley (see footnote 2). His sons were active in the Regulator movement and the Whig militia. Orange County Wills, A-53; Clerk of Superior Court, Hillsborough, N. C. Saunders, *Colonial Records*, VII, 734–35, 758–67.

sent out spies. in the Course of 2 hours one of my spies gave me information of a party of Rebels plundering his house which was about three miles off. I instantly marched to the place and Discovered them in a field near the house. I attacked them Immediately and Kept up a smart fire for half an hour, during which time we Killed their Capt and one private on the spot, wounded three of them and took two prisoners besides 8 of their horses well appointed and several swords, this happened on the 11th of May, 1781.— the same day we pursued another party of Rebels and came up with them. the morning following we attacked them smartly and Killed 4 of them on the spot, wounded 3 dangerously and took one prisoner with all their horses and appointments. in about an hour after that we took two men of the same party and Killed one more of them—the same Evening we had Intelligence of another party of Rebels which where assembling about 30 miles off in order for to attack us. as I thought it best to surprise them where they where collecting I marched all night and about 10 o'Clock next morning we came up with them. we commenced a fire upon each other which continued for about 10 minutes when they Retreated. We Killed two of them and wounded 7 and took 18 horses well appointed. We then Returned to Deep River again. I still Kept the Company together and waited for another opportunity during which time I took two Rebel soldiers and parolled them, who gave me information of a Col^n Dudley[57] Coming from General Greens Camp at Cambden[58] with Baggage. I mounted my men and set forward in search of them, and I concealed my men by the side of the Road and I thought the time long according to Information I had from the soldiers. I took one man with me and went to see if I could make any discovery. I Rode a mile and a half when I saw Col^n Dudley with his baggage. I then wheeld my horse and Returned to my men, when I came within a hundred yards of them Dudley and his Dragoons was nose and Tail, and snaped their pistols several times. I then ordered a march after them and after marching 2½ miles I discovered them and immediately took 3 of them prisoners and all the Baggage with 9 horses, the Baggage I divided amongst my men which agreeably to Colonel Dudleys Report was vallued at £1000 sterling. I Returned to Coxes Mill and Remained there untill 8th of June when the Rebels embodied 160 men to attack me under the

[57] GUILFORD DUDLEY raised a volunteer company and served in the Moore's Creek Bridge campaign. He was at Camden and later with Greene in South Carolina. By 1781 he was colonel of light horse from the Cumberland County militia and in September was serving in Virginia. Clark, *State Records*, XVII, 586–87, 1039; XVIII, 17. Wynne and Wheeler, *Fanning's Narrative*, p. 76n.

[58] Camden, South Carolina, formerly a fortified British outpost, was now under American control.

Command of Col^n Collyer[59] and Balfour.[60]—I Determined to get the advantage of attacking them which I Did with 49 men in the night after marching 10 miles to their Encampment. they took one of my Guides which gave them notice of my approach. I proceeded within thirty steps of them but being unacquainted with the Ground advanced very cautiously. the centinel however discovered my party and firing upon us and Retreated in, when they secured themselves under cover of the houses and fences.— firing then began and continued on both Sides for the Space of 4 Hours being very cloudy and Dark during which time I had one man Killed and 6 wounded and the guide before mentioned taken prisoner whom they Killed the next morning in Cold Blood.—what Injury they Suffered I could not learn.—as the morning appeared we Retreated and Returned again to Deep River leaving our wounded men at a friends house privately. the Rebels then Kept a constant Scouting and their numbers was so Great that we had to lay still for some time and when Collier & Belfour left the settlement the said Col^n Dudley before mentioned took place with 300 men from Virginia and took a negro man from me and sould him at public Auction amongst themselves for 110 pound. the said negro was sent over the mountains and I never saw him since. at length they all began to scatter and we to embody, and Wm Elrood[61] being jelous of my taking too much

[59] A key adversary of Fanning, JOHN COLLIER served as a justice of the peace from Guilford County in 1776 and was a justice for the newly formed Randolph County 1779–87. He was appointed colonel of the Randolph County militia in 1779 and resigned in May, 1782. He represented Guilford County in the House of Commons in 1777 and was in the state senate from Randolph County four sessions, 1779–82. Randolph County Court Minutes, March, 1779; Division of Archives and History, Raleigh, N. C. Clark, *State Records*, XVI, 148, 203–5; XX, 186; XXIII, 994. John L. Cheney, Jr. (ed.), *North Carolina Government, 1584–1974: A Narrative and Statistical History* (Raleigh, N. C.: North Carolina Department of the Secretary of State, 1975), pp. 201, 204, 206, 207, 209.

[60] ANDREW BALFOUR, a merchant from Edinburgh, Scotland, came to New England in 1772. He moved south in 1777 to join his brother in Charleston. By July, 1778 he was in Salisbury, North Carolina, and had purchased a 1900-acre plantation in the present Randolph County. He was a justice of the peace of the newly formed Randolph County in 1779 and by 1781 was lieutenant colonel of the Whig county militia. He was assassinated by Fanning on March 11, 1782. His sister, Margaret Balfour, who was a witness of the murder, testified at Hillsborough in April, 1783, against Frederick Smith, who was convicted of aiding Fanning in the death of Balfour and was hanged. Balfour represented his county in the House of Commons in the sessions of 1780 and 1781. Clark, *State Records*, XV, 555; XVI, 244–45; XX, 263–64. Cheney, *North Carolina Government*, pp. 206, 208. Randolph County Court Minutes, June 1779; December, 1779; June, 1781; Division of Archives and History, Raleigh, N. C. Caruthers, *Revolutionary Incidents*, pp. 297–343, *passim*. Ashe, *Biographical History*, II, 17–19.

[61] WILLIAM ELROD from the forks of the Yadkin River apparently had an independent command and challenged Fanning's leadership. According to Caruthers he was a major in the militia and was killed in March, 1782, by Whigs. Caruthers, *Revolutionary Incidents*, pp. 344–58.

Command of the men, and in my absence one Day he pursuaded them that I was a Going to make them Regular Soldiers and Cause them to be attached to Col^n John Hammiltons Rigement and Vindicated it by an advertisement that I had handed to several of the Loyalists that I thought had the Greatest Influence with the Loyalists. he so prevailed with the common sorts that when I came to camp I found the most of my men gone.—I then declared I never would go on another Scoute untill there was a field officer and the majority Chose me. they then drew up a petion to the Commanding Officer of the Kings troops—

Then a General meeting of the Loyalist was now called in order for to appoint a Cammanding Officer of the Militia. it was still determined I should be the person.—I accordingly Set off for Wilmington being 160 miles with a——petion of the people to the Officer commanding at that post for his approbation.—on my arrival there Major Craig[62] who commanded treated me with Every Respect in his power and approved of said petion and gave a Commission as Col^n of the Randolph and chatham Counties Militia, a copy of which is hereunto annexed

By James Henry Craigg. Esqr Major in his Majesties 82^d Rigement Commanding a detachment of the Kings troops in North Carolina &c., &c.

To David Fanning. Esqr

These are to appoint you to be Colonel of the Loyal Militia of Randolph and Chatham Counties who are Directed to obey you as such in all lawfull Commands whatsoever and you are authorised to Grant Commissions to the necessary persons of Known attachment to his majestys person and Government to act as Cap^{tns} and Subalterns to the different Companyes of militia aforesaid—as Colonel you are hereby fully enpowerd to assemble the militia and lead them against any parties of Rebels or others the King's

---

[62] Sir JAMES HENRY CRAIG (1748-1812) was from Gibraltar and entered the army in 1763 as an ensign. He was promoted to captain in the 47th regiment in 1771 and accompanied this regiment to American in 1774. He was wounded in his first action at Bunker's Hill and was transferred with his regiment to Canada in 1776. Twice wounded in Burgoyne's invasion of New York, he was promoted to major in the newly formed 82nd regiment. His excellent record while in command of the post at Wilmington led to the rank of lieutenant colonel of the 82nd regiment. After the Revolution he remained in the army, and during the Napoleonic Wars his distinguished service in difficult commands resulted in his achieving the rank of lieutenant general by 1801. An able administrator, he was appointed governor-general of Canada, serving successfully from 1807 until 1811. Leslie Stephen and Sidney Lee (eds.), *The Dictionary of National Biography* (London: Oxford University Press, 1917), IV, 1368–70.

enemies as often as necessary, to compel all persons whatever to join you and to seize and disarm and when necessary to detain in Confinement all Rebels or others acting against his Majesties Government and to do all other acts becomeing a Kings Officer and Good Subject. Given at Wilmington this 5th of July, 1781—

> Signed J. H. Craigg. Major
> Commanding the Kings Troops

on the 12 of July I Returned from Wilmington and ordered a General Muster and then gave the following Commission to the Gentlemen hereafter named of their Respective Companies—

By David Fanning Esq[r] Colonel of the Loyal Militia of North Carolina

   To   Greeting—
Having Received Suffient testimony of your Loyalty and Zeal for his Majesties service and Relying on your courage and Good conduct I do hereby appoint you to be   of a Company in the District of   you are therefore diligently and carefully to discharge the duty of such obeying all orders and directions which you may Receive from time to time from any superior officers in his Majesties service and all others, the Inferior officers of his Majesties Subjects of that and every other Company are Directed and Requested to obey you as   of the Said company. Given under my hand at Coxes Mill this   1781.

> David Fanning Colonel.
> Commanding his Majesties Loyal Militia, &c.

The names of the officers of Randolph County as they was Commissioned in their Different Companies.

1 John Rains,[63] Captain	16th of July	promoted Maj[r] 13 of Oct[br] 1781			
William Rains, Lieu[t]	in N. C.	Do.	Cap[t]	do.	do
Thomas Dannelly Ensig[n]	died in Charelston	do.	Lieu[t]	do	do

[63] The Rains family of Randolph and Chatham counties provided several Loyalist officers for Fanning's command. Fanning cited in the journal the important services of his second-in-command Major John Rains and of Captain George Rains. JOHN and GEORGE RAINS of Orange County (late Randolph and Chatham) signed Regulator petitions in 1768, and John Rains was mentioned in the Chatham County Court Minutes, November, 1777. Division of Archives and History, Raleigh, N. C. Saunders, *Colonial Records*, VII, 734–35. John Rains lived on Brush Creek in western Chatham County near the Randolph County

John Spinks[64] Serg.^t Major		do Ensign do do

2 George Rains Captain.	16th of July 1781	in Charlston at the peace
Ebenezer Wollaston. Lieu.^t	do.	
Robert Rains Ensign	do.	in N. Carolina

3 William Fincannon Capt	2^d of August 1781	now in North Carolina
Richard Bird Lieu.^t	do.	do.
Cornelious Lathem Ensign	do.	do novm.^r 1789

4 Michael Robins Capt	2^d of Augt 1781	last account in N. C.
William Hillis Lieu.^t	do.	went to East Florida at the peace
Daniel Brown Ensign	do.	Killed by the Rebels in N. C.

5 Robert Turner Capt	2^d of Aug.st 1781	last account in N. C.
Absolum Autery Lieu.^t	do	in East Florida at the peace
William King. Ensign	do	joined the Rebels

6 Stephen Walker Capt	17th of Sep.^{tm} 1781	shot Catched wounded & then murdered
Frederick Smith[65] Lieu.^t	do.	hanged at Hilsborough for his Loyalty
William Huntsucker Ensign	do	do. do.

7 Joseph Currie, Capt	17 of Sept.^m 1781	in East florida at the peace
Benjamin Shields Lieu.^t	do	in North Carolina do.
James Rains Ensign	do	in the mountains S. C. do.

line. Murphey Notes. In 1790 a John, George, Robert, and William Reines, as well as other Reines households, were living in Randolph County. *Heads of Families at the First Census of the United States in the Year 1790: North Carolina* (Baltimore, Md.: Genealogical Publishing Co., reprint edition, 1966), p. 99.

[64] In 1790 John Spinks, Richard Bird, Cornelius Lathem, and Harry Ramsower (see above) were living in Randolph County with their families. Lathem and Bird had one slave each. *1790 Census*, p. 99.

[65] See footnote 60 on the execution of Frederick Smith. Caruthers, *Revolutionary Incidents*, pp. 325–29.

The names of the officers of the different Companies in Chatham County.

8 Thomas Dark[66] Cap[t]	16th of July 1781	hanged in Hilsborough for his Loyalty
William Hoocker Lieu[t]	do.	murdered by the Rebels after pro[m] Capt.
Henry Ramssower Ensign	do	promoted Lieutenant at Charles town at peace
9 William Lindley.[67] Cap[t]	16th of July 1781	murdered by the Rebels at the mountains
William Piles Lieu[t]	do.	went to penselvania
William M[c]Pherson Ensign	do	in Charles town at the avacuation
10 Samuel Dark.[68] Cap[t]	16th of July 1781	last account in North Carolina
James Ellett. Lieu[t]	do	drowned in East Florida
Thomas Ellett. Ensign	do	in East Florida at the peace.
11 Benjamin Underwood Cap[t]	1st of Sept 1781	late in N. Brunswick
Fredrick Smith Lieu[t]	do.	in N. C.
Adam Smith Ensign	do	in N. C.
12 William Deaton Cap[t]	1st of Sep[t] 1781	Killed in Battle the day after the Rebel Governor Burk was taken
William Carr. Lieu[t]	do	promt Cap[t] now in N. providence West Indies 28th of Nov. 1789

[66] Caruthers printed the Hillsborough district court record of January 17, 1782, of the sentence of Thomas Dark, Thomas Estridge, Meredith Edwards, Thomas Rickets, Samuel Poe, William Duke, and Thomas Hunt. Dark, Estridge, and Edwards were convicted of high treason and hanged. Unless there were two Loyalists named Meredith Edwards, Fanning was mistaken about Edwards being in East Florida. Caruthers, *Revolutionary Incidents*, pp. 251–53.

[67] WILLIAM LINDLEY, the son of James Lindley (see footnote 2), had settled in Chatham County by August, 1774. He commanded a company raiding in Orange County in August, 1781. Fanning entrusted him with several important missions mentioned in the journal. His murder by Loyalist deserters in early 1782 is described in the journal. Clark, *State Records*, XXII, 1047. Caruthers, *Revolutionary Incidents*, pp. 142, 256. Hoyt, *Murphey Papers*, II, 296–397. Chatham County Deeds, A, 367; microfilm; Division of Archives and History, Raleigh, N. C.

[68] SAMUEL DARK purchased 18 acres on Landrum's Creek of Rocky River in Chatham County in September, 1772. Chatham County Deeds, A, 130; Register of Deeds, Pittsboro, N. C. He was living in Chatham County in 1790. *1790 Census*, p. 87.

John Ervin Ensign	do	promt'd Capt of T. Darks comp^y now in E. Florida

13 Martin Kendrick[69] Capt	1st of Sep^t 1781	in N. Carolina
Thomas McDowel Lieu^t	do	now Rebel Captain Nov^{mb} 29th 1789
William Brown Ensign	do.	Joined the Rebels

The names of the officers in the different Companies in Orange County.—

14 Richard Edwards Capt	16th of July 1781	Killed in Battle
Edward Edwards Lieu^t	do.	promoted Capt. Killed the 13th of Sep^t in Battle
Thomas Estrich Ensign	do	prom^{td} Capt the Day after

15 Stephen Holloway. Capt	16th of July 1781	Killed in Battle
John Hastings[70] Lieu^t	do	in N. Carolina
Abraham Nelson Ensign	do	wounded and now in N. C.

The names of the officers in the different Companies in Cumberland County —

16 John Cagle. Capt	16th of July 1781	hanged by the Rebels at P. d.
Jacob Manness Lieut.	do	in N. Carolina
William Dunn Ensign	do	in N. C.

17 Meriday Edwards. Capt	1st of Sept. 1781	in E. Florida at the peace
Reuben Shields[71] Lieu^t	do.	in N. C.
William Hancock Ensign	do	in N. C

18 Alx^r McIver. Capt	1st of August 1781	in N. C.
Murdick Martin Lieu^t	do	in N. providence or England

19 William M^{c}loud Capt	2^d of Augst 1781	went to Europe
Alx^r M^{c}loud Lieu^t	do.	went to Europe

[69] In 1790 MARTIN KENDRICK was living in Chatham County. *1790 Census*, p. 85.
[70] In 1790 JOHN HASTINGS was living in Orange County. *1790 Census*, p. 95.
[71] In 1790 REUBEN SHIELDS was living in Stokes County. *1790 Census*, p. 181.

The names of the officers of the Companys in Anson County

20 William Price Cap[t]	2[d] of Aug[st] 1781	Killed by the Rebels
William Fanning, Lieut	do.	hanged by do.

21 William Knight Cap[t]	16th of July 1781	murdered by the Rebels
Stephen Phillips Lieu[t]	do.	in S. C.

22 Abner Smally[72] Cap[t]	in Birk County in the mountains
	in East Florida at the peace
Joseph Hodge Lieu[t]	murdered by the Rebels

Those gentlemen had their appointments from Major Forgeson in South Carolina in July 1780   Joined all of them accordin to the Dates.

On my Return to Deep River I immediately caused a General Muster of the Loyalists which I collected to the amount of 150 men but finding them deficiont in arms I dischargd all of them except 53, which I appointed fully out of which I collected from the whole; and ordered the rest to be Ready to Join me when I called for them. I also gave the foregoing commissions to the different officers set fourth who Rendered many Services to the British Government during The late war, who Singulared themselves with me in the Interior parts of that Rebellious Country and Subdued the greatest part of the province so far, that the worst of Rebels came to me beging protection for themselves and Property—the Exertions of myself and the other officers had the whole Country under the protection of British Government intill long after the surrender of Lord Cornwallis and the Evacuation of Wilmington and after all the British Troops was called to their different posts on the sea shore I continued acting in the interior parts of N. Carolina and was like to obtain a truse with the Rebels in the heart of the Country.— Those people has been Interduced to abrave every danger and Difficulty during the late war. Rather then to Render any service to the Rebels—had their Properties Real and personal taken to seport their Enimies—the fatherless and widows striped and Every manner of seport taken from them, their houses and lands and all personal property taken and no Restin place could be found for them—as to place them in their former Possions it is Impossible—striped of their property, Drove from their homes, deprived of their wives and children, Robbed of a free and mild Government,

[72] In 1790 ABNER SMALLY was living in Burke County. *1790 Census*, p. 109.

betrayed and deserted by their friends, what can Repay them for their misery. Dragged out a wretched life of obscurity and want, heaven only which Smoothe the Rugged paths can Reconcile them to misfortunes.

Numbers of them left their wives and children in North Carolina, their being not able to send for them, owing to the Distresses and now in the West Indies and other parts of the world for Refuge and not Returned to their families Yett, and some of them that Returned under the Act of ablivion passed in 1783,[73] was taken and Sent to Hilsborough and hanged for their past services that they Rendered Government whilst under my command. —I am fully sencible of the Good Designs that Government Intends for the Loyalists in so Repeatedly Renewing the Act, if the Innibility and Distressed situation of those people who have Suffered and Experienced Every thing But Death to seport British Government and Cannot Reap the fruits of their labour, and now poin under Every Species of mortification. I can solmnly Declare that I think Major John Rains and Capt George Rains two of the Deserveings officers that Ever acted in America During the late war, Either in the provential or Militia and to my Certain Knowledge John Rains had two mills Burnt, three Dwelling. houses besides a barn and property totally taken away. I have Given a Direct account of the officers opposite their names as I possibly can, also of their promotions and Deaths, what I have Set forth I will forever vindicate.—Besides other officers of other counties that Joined me at Different times and plases as I shall Refer to the other parts of my Journal, in Particular Col^n Arch^{bl} McDugald[74] and Saml Andrews[75] who joined me several times. Given at Kings County New Brunswick Nov^m 29th 1789.

---

[73] The Act of Pardon and Oblivion of 1783 pardoned all acts of treason since July 4, 1776, but excluded all crown officers, all persons named in confiscation acts, all citizens who had left the state to go to the British and had not returned, and those guilty of murder, robbery, rape, or arson. Fanning, Samuel Andrews, and Peter Mallett were specifically excluded. Clark, *State Records*, XXIV, 489–90.

[74] ARCHIBALD MCDUGALD, a native of Scotland, settled in Cumberland County by 1767. In 1779 he attempted to join the British at Savannah but was captured and held a prisoner at Charleston. He escaped and became an ensign in the Royal North Carolina Regiment, serving in the Southern campaign. At Wilmington in 1781 he was appointed colonel of the Cumberland County militia by Major Craig. He went with Craig to Charleston and then with the British evacuation to East Florida. He was in Country Harbour, Nova Scotia, in 1786. Loyalist Claim (North Carolina): Archibald McDugald. Troxler, "Migrations of Loyalists," p. 217.

[75] SAMUEL ANDREWS from near New Bern, North Carolina, was appointed a lieutenant of militia by Governor Josiah Martin and was captured at Moore's Creek Bridge in February, 1776. He was released that fall after taking a state loyalty oath. In 1781 he raised a company of Loyal Militia in Bladen County and rode with Fanning. The next year he was in Charleston with the rank of major. He was one of three Loyalists specifically excluded from

The Rebels the same day held a General Muster at Chatham Court house[76] about 25 miles from where I had assembled, and the day following were for to call a Court Martial for the trial of Several Loyalists who had Refused to bear arms in opposition to Government. upon Receiving this Intelligence I proceeded towards the Court Hous 17 miles that night with the men I had armed—and the morning following by 7 o'clock arrived there. I surrounded the place where I Expected to find members of the Court Martial But they had dispersed the Evening before and were for to meet at 8 oclock. I then posted picketts on Every Road and within the space of two hours took 53 prisoners Amongst which was the Col[n] Major and all the Militia officers of the County Except two who had not attended and also one Continental Cap[t] with 3 of the Deligates of their Assembly. I immediately marched them to Coxes Mill and Paroled them all Except 14 who I Knew where Violent against Government, those I conducted to Wilmington and delivered to Major Craigg.

I then Represented to Major Craigg that with his approbation I would establish certain Regulations for the conduct of the militia which he approved off and was oblidging Enough on my giving them to him to convict and confirm the following Rules which where in a short time after that had printed and distributed in the country—

Rules and Regulations for the well Governing the Loyal Militia of the province of North Carolina—
1st No person for to be admitted a militia man untill he takes the oath of allegiance to his Majesty which is allways to be done before three Senior Officers of the Regiment on the spot.
2[d] all persons once Enrolled in a militia Company and having taken the Oath abovementioned will be Considered as Entitled to every priviledge and protection of a British Subject, and will on being detected joining the Rebels will be treated as a Deserter and Traitor—
3[d] Every militia man is to Repair without fail or Excuse Except Sickness at the time appointed to the place assigned by his Col[n] or Cap[t] with his arms and accoutrements and is not to quit his Company on any pretence whatever, without the Knowledge and permission of his Captain or Commanding Officer—
4th The Colonel of every County has full power to Call his Regiment

the North Carolina Act of Pardon and Oblivion of 1783. When Charleston was evacuated he went to East Florida and finally was in Shelburne, Nova Scotia, by 1785. Sabine, *Loyalist Sketches*, I, 165–66. Troxler, "Migration of Loyalists," p. 196. DeMond, *Loyalists*, p. 237.

[76] Chatham Courthouse is the present town of Pittsboro. The raid on Chatham Courthouse occurred on July 17, 1781. The Whig accounts substantiate Fanning's narrative. Hoyt, *Murphey Papers*, II, 389. Clark, *State Records*, XXII, 550.

together and march them when necessary for his Majesties service, the Capt of Each Company has also power to assemble his Company when any Sudden Emergency Renders it necessary and which he is to Report as soon after as possible to his Colonel.

5th Mutual assistance is to be given on all occations But as it is impossible to give positive Directions on this subject, it is left to the discretion of Colonels of Regiments who must be answerable that their Reasons for not affording assistance when Required are sufficient.

6th when the militia of different Counties are Embodied the senior officer is to Command Colonels of Regiments are Immediately to determine the present Rank of their Cap^{ts} in which Regard is to be had to Seniority of Commission or Service—in Caces of Vacancies Colonels may Grant temporary Commissions till Recourse can be had to the commanding officer of the Kings Troops.—

7th the men are to understand that in what Relates to the service they are bound to Obey all officers tho' not immediately belonging to their own Companies—

8th Courts Martial may Sit by the Appointment of the Colonel or Commanding Officer and must Consist for the trial of an officer of all the officers of the Regiment he belongs to Except the Colonel or Commanding Officer and for the trial of a non Commissioned officer or private man of 2 Captains 2 Subalterns and 3 private men, the latter to belong to the same Company as the person to be tried: the oldest Capt to preside and the sentence of the Court to be determined by plurality of Votes and approved of by the Commanding Officer—

9th No Colonel is to supercede an officer without trial but he may suspend him till he can be tried——

10th Quiting Camp without permission, Disobedience of Orders neglect of duty plundering and all Irrugalarities and disorders subversive of Good order and discipline are to be punished at the discretion of a Court martial—Constituted as above mentioned and by the approbation of the Colonel or Commanding Officer, who has power to pardon or Remit any part of a punishment but not to Encrease or alter it——

11th Every man must take the Greatest care of his arms and ammunition and have them always Ready for service——

12th when the militia is not Embodied they are at all times to be attentive to the motions of the Rebels and Emediately to acquaint the nearest officer of any thing may Discover who is to communicate it to his Colonel or other Officers as may be Requisite——

13th It is the duty of every person professing allegiance to his Majesty to communicate to the commanding officer of the nearest British post every intiligence he can procure of the assembling or moveing of any bodies of Rebels, persons employed on this occation shall always be paid.

14th Colonels of Regiments may assemble any number of their men which they may think necessary to be posted in particular spots of their Districts their time of service on these occations is to be limited and they are at the Expiration of it to be Relieved by others.—Great Care is to be taken that no partiality is shown but that each take an equal proportion of duty, for which purpose Alphebatical Rolls are to be Kept by which the men are to be warned.—Every Captain is to Keep an account of the number of days each man of his Company serves.

The strict observeance of the Above Regulations is Strongly Recommended as the best means of the Kings faithful subjects a manifest superiority over the Rebel militia and ensure them that success their Zeal and Spirit in the cause of their Country entitles them to Expect.—

Head Quarters Wilmington. 25th Sep[m] 1781.

I then thought it prudent to administer the following Oath of Allegiance unto those people I was dubious of—

I A. B. do Swear on the holy evangelists of almighty God to bear true allegiance to our sovereign Lord King George the third and to uphold the same. I do voluntarily promise for to serve as militia under any of the officers appointed over me and that I will when Lawfully warned by our said officers assemble at any place by them Directed in case of danger, in the space of 8 hours, I will Go with my arms and accoutrements in Good order to Suppress any Rebels or others the Kings enemies, that I will not at any time Do or cause to be done any thing prejudicial to his majesties Government or suffer any Intercourse or Correspondence with the Enemies thereof, that I will make Known any plot or plots any wise Inimical to his Majestyes forces or loyal subjects by me Discovered to any of his Majesties Officers contiguous, and it shall not exceed six hours before the said is discovered, if health and distance permit this. I do solemnly swear and promice to defend in all cases whatsoever.—so help me God

I then Returned to the head of Little River[77] on my way to Coxes Mill, where I was met by two men who Informed me that the Rebels had seperated into small parties thinking I should never Return from Wilming-

---

[77] Although there are several Little Rivers in North Carolina, Fanning is clearly referring here to the Little River that arises in southwestern Moore County and flows through Cumberland County to the Cape Fear.

ton. I passed and got Intelligence of Colonel Alstine[78] lying on the banks of Deep River. with a party of 25 men we marched all that day and that night following and just as the day Dawned we advanced in three divisions up to a house they had thrown themselves into on our approach. we fired upon the house as I was determined for to make Example of them for behaving in the manner they had done to one of my pilots by name Kenneth Black.[79] they Returned our fire and the Action continued upwards of 3 hours when after Killing 4 of them and wounding all the Rest except 3, they sent out a flag to Surrender Col[n] Alstines Lady begging their lives, and on her Solicitation I concluded to grant her Request—

and after the Capitulation I gave the following Paroals to Col[n] Philip Alstine and his men—

I do hereby acknowledge myself a prisoner of War. upon my Parole to his Excellency Si[r] Henry Clinton and that I am hereby engaged till I shall be exchanged or otherwise Released therefrom to Proceed Emediately to my plantation on Dunnams Creek Cumberland County or elsewhere N[or] Carolina there to Remain or within five miles thereof and that I shall not in the mean time do or Cause any thing to be done prejuditial to the success of his Majesties arms or have Intercourse or hold Correspondence with the inemies of his Majesty, and that upon a Summons from his Excellency or other Persons having authority thereto that I will surrender myself up to him or them at such time & place as shall hereafter be Required——

Cumberland County Deep River July 29th 1781

Philip Alstine Col[n]

Witness

David Fanning, Col[n] Com[d] Loyal Militia

[78] PHILIP ALSTON purchased in Cumberland County (now Moore County) 4,000 acres on the Deep River in 1772 and was the first owner of the "House in the Horseshoe." Within five years he had accumulated 6,525 acres and was a county justice. In 1776 he was appointed lieutenant colonel of the county militia and succeeded to colonel in 1778. Captured at Briar Creek, Georgia, in 1779, he escaped from a prison ship and returned home to lead the militia against Fanning. On May 23, 1781, he was appointed by the governor to be colonel of an independent partisan corps. Alston was ruthless toward his opponents. A contemporary, Robert Rowan, wrote of him that he "seems to rule them all, and a greater tyrant is not upon the earth. . . ." When Moore County was created in 1784 he became a justice and the first clerk of court. He was elected to the state senate 1785–86. Accused of murder while in the senate, he was pardoned by the governor. Accusations of various crimes by a local rival, George Glascock, led to Alston's being suspended as a county justice in December, 1787, and a few months later Glascock was murdered. Following this incident Alston was arrested several times for contempt of court and as an accessory to the murder. He escaped from the Wilmington jail in 1790 and was presumably murdered in Tennessee in 1791. Blackwell P. Robinson, *A History of Moore County, North Carolina, 1747–1847* (Southern Pines, N. C.: Moore County Historical Association, 1956), pp. 16, 65, 92, 107, 111–17. Jo White Linn and B. R. McBride, " Delamar Revolutionary Pension Abstracts," *North Carolina Geneaological Society Journal*, II (April, 1976), 108. Clark, *State Records*, XI, 629.

In the course of the affair we had 2 men Killed and 4 Wounded who afterwards Recovered.—A party of Rebels appeared in sight a little time after the firing began but did not approach to afford Col^n Alstine any support.[80] when the action was over they ran off and our horses being quite fatigued Rendered it impossible for me to pursue them and I then pursued my Route to Coxes Mill where on my arrival I gave 12 hours leave to the men, after detaining a sufficient number for the necessary Guards, to go to their Respective homes. Immediately after I heard that a waggon loaded with Salt for the use of the Rebel army had passed about 12 hours; I took 8 men with me and after a Chace of 16 miles I overtook *her* and Conducted it back to Coxes Mill. On my Return I found Major Rains had been attacked by a party of 150 Rebels who had attempted to secure the Fort of Deep River at Coxes Mill. however it was without success, he had one man wounded and Several horses in the Attack, and on my approach they Retreated.—they then sent a flag with officers of peace. I returned for—Answer, I was determined to make peace with the Sword or otherwise they should become subjects to Great Britain. My men now being Collected to the amount of— 140, who by this time were well armed and hearing nothing further from thence the next morning marched to the place I had been informed they were but found them gone off. I discovered some of their scouts. but firing on them they took to the woods. I heard they had marched and joined another party of 250 men Commanded by Colonels Paisley[81] and Balfour, upon which I Returned to Coxes Mill. I sent out spies that night who

[79] KENNETH BLACK, a native of Jura, Scotland, came to North Carolina about 1740 but did not establish his residence in Cumberland County in the section that is now Moore County until 1772. Influential among the Highland Scots, Black's home was the refuge of Flora MacDonald and her family for nearly two years. Caruthers has a detailed account of the death of Black by Philip Alston's men in July, 1781, which led directly to the encounter between Fanning and Alston at the House in the Horseshoe. Clark, *State Records*, XXII, 550. Robinson, *Moore County*, pp. 35n., 40–41, 68, 71–73, 76, 78. Caruthers, *Revolutionary Incidents*, pp. 181–82, 390.

[80] General John Butler's report is the source of the accepted date of August 5 for the skirmish at the House in the Horseshoe, but Butler was apparently off a week. The dated parole included in the text is a better source. Murphey adds that the surrender was forced by Fanning's preparation to burn the house. One of Fanning's dead was a British officer who attempted to lead a frontal assault on the house. He is identified by Murphey as Captain Andrews and by Caruthers as Lieutenant McKay. Murphey names Captain Duck (see footnote 53) as the leader of the Whig reinforcement. Clark, *State Records*, XXII, 557; Hoyt, *Murphey Papers*, II, 395–96; Caruthers, *Revolutionary Incidents*, pp. 180–90; Robinson, *Moore County*, pp. 78–82.

[81] JOHN PAISLEY (d. 1811) of Brush Creek in Guilford County acquired over 1000 acres during and after the Revolution. He was appointed a major of minutemen in September, 1775, and lieutenant colonel of the county militia in April, 1776. Very active in the course of the war, he served in the Cherokee campaign in Georgia in 1778, in the Southern campaign of General Greene, at Guilford Courthouse, and in numerous forays against the Loyalists.

Returned before morning and Informed me that the two Rebel parties had joined, being about 400 in number and encamped at Browns plantation about 2 miles up the River. on the opposite side. I dispatched a flag to them acquainting them as before of my determination in support of Government and proposed a meeting of both parties to determine the matter by [force] of arms, at the same time acquainting them that the ill treatment of some prisoners they had taken a little time before had determined me to Retaliate in case and end was not put to it, and any in future have cause to complain. I directed the flag to Major Cage[82] who Commanded at the time before, and I Received the following answer—

Si[r]—I Received yours by a flag and can Inform you that I should be as sorry as any person Living to mis-use a prisoner, but at the same time I think it my duty to oppose my Enemies and if any of your men should fall into my hands I shall endeavour to use what influence I can to have them treated as prisoners and I hope you will do the same. I must also inform you that I am not the commanding officer, if I was—I Should Immediately Return You an answer and as your letters was not Directed to the Commanding officer he will not undertake it without you will direct to him. Col[n] ONeal[83] Commands at present.

I am yours, &c., &c.,

Wm. Cage

To Col[n] David Fanning august the 2[d] 1781

I also Recv[d] a message from Col: O.Neal that whereever they met me they would fight me, but not by an Immediate appointment.—I directly ordered a march and proceeded to the place where I was informed by the Bearer of the flag they lay encamped, but on my arrival there they had marched off, and from Inteligence I had procured. I had Reason to suppose they *was* gone to Salisbury to get Reinforced by General Ruther-

---

In 1782 he was one of the commissioners of confiscated estates for Guilford County. Saunders, *Colonial Records*, X, 206, 351, 355. Clark, *State Records*, XIV, 616, 692; XXII, 144, 146, 151. Guilford County Deeds and Wills, Greensboro, N. C.

[82] WILLIAM CAGE received a state grant of 400 acres on Dry Creek, Chatham County, in November, 1779. He was a captain in the county militia and was promoted to major in July, 1781. He was captured by the Loyalists in August. After the war he moved west to the territory that became Tennessee and represented Sullivan County in the North Carolina House of Commons in 1783 and 1784. Clark, *State Records*, XV, 557; XIX, 855; XXII, 557, 571, 585. Cheney, *North Carolina Government*, pp. 212, 213. Chatham County Deeds, B, 201; Register of Deeds, Pittsboro, N. C.

[83] WILLIAM O'NEAL lived on Haw River in Orange County and was a major and then colonel of the county militia. He resigned as colonel in 1790. Clark, *State Records*, XVI, 211, 244; XXI, 974; XXII, 557, 575. Orange County Deeds, III, 40, 348; IV, 369; Register of Deeds, Hillsborough. N. C.

ford.[84] I then concluded to go to Wilmington for a supply of Ammunition finding my stock began for to grow low. I got to Cross Creek on the 11th of August and early on the morning following Crossed Cape Fear. When Major Samuel Andrews joined me with his Company and scouted through all the Rebel Settlements on the North side of the River and took a number of prisoners arms & horses.

I also discovered where 25 Barrells of Salt was Concealed designed for the Rebel army. I destroyed it and then marched down the side of the River and Came to a plantation belonging to a Capt Robertson[85] which I Burned—from thence I marched to his Brother Col^n Robertsons[86] which I served in the same manner. on my march I took Several prisoners whom I paroled except 20. those I delivered to Capt Legett,[87] then Commanding at Wilmington where I arrived on the 24th. having got supplied with ammuni-

[84] GRIFFITH RUTHERFORD (1731-1800), a native of Ireland, was in Rowan County by 1753. He served in the General Assembly in 1766, 1770, 1771–74 and as county sheriff in 1769. He was a captain of militia in the War of the Regulation in 1771. A delegate to the provincial congresses of 1775 and 1776, he was appointed colonel of the county militia in September, 1775. Promoted to brigadier general of the western district in April, 1776, he commanded the force that ravaged the Cherokee nation the following summer. Beginning in 1777 he was in the state senate for most of the sessions until 1786. Rutherford was wounded and captured at the battle of Camden in August, 1780, and exchanged a year later. He commanded the militia in the Wilmington Expedition that cleared the lower Cape Fear of the British in the fall of 1781. In 1786 he moved to the territory that became Tennessee. Ashe, *Biographical History*, II, 381–85.

[85] PETER ROBESON of Bladen County was a member of the Committee of Safety and a captain in the county militia, serving throughout the war. He was in the House of Commons two terms in the period 1784–87, and was major of militia for the Wilmington District in 1787. He was the brother of Colonel Thomas Robeson. Cheney, *North Carolina Government*, p. 214. Clark, *State Records*, XV, 737–38; XVIII, 449. Leora H. McEachern and Isabel M. Williams (eds.), *Wilmington-New Hanover Safety Committee Minutes, 1774–1776* (Wilmington: Wilmington-New Hanover American Revolution Bi-centennial Association, 1974), pp. 45, 132.

[86] THOMAS ROBESON of Bladen County was colonel of the Whig militia and a key antagonist of the Cape Fear valley Loyalists. He was a member of the county Committee of Safety in 1775 and represented his county in the provincial congresses of 1776. In 1777 he served as a state senator from Bladen. Robeson County, North Carolina, is named for him. Cheney, *North Carolina Government*, pp. 156, 158, 201. Clark, *State Records*, XV, 438, 542–43; XVI, 487, 717; XXII, 543–44, 546–47. MCeachern and Williams, *Safety Committee Minutes*, pp. 45, 132.

[87] JOHN LEGGETT of Bladen County raised a company in the Moore's Creek Bridge campaign where he was captured and held prisoner for two years. He was exchanged at New York but recaptured and exchanged after the fall of Charleston in May, 1780. He received a commission as a provincial captain in September, 1778, and the next year joined the Royal North Carolina Regiment and served under Major Craig at Wilmington. In August, 1780, he was in command of the forces at Wilmington. His property was confiscated in 1779. After the evacuation of Charleston he went to East Florida, and by 1786 he was in Country Harbour, Nova Scotia. Loyalist Claim (North Carolina): John Leggett, Troxler, "Migra-

tion I proceeded up the Country on the 26th on my march to Elizabeth town where on my arrival I found Coln. Slingsbee[88] of the Loyal Militia of Bladen County—with a number of paroled Rebels—in his camp. I disapproved of Keeping them there and told him I thought it imprudent and unsafe, the Event proved so, for that night they having arms Concealed fired upon *his camp* and wounded him mortally and five Captains also were wounded some of which died afterwards of their wounds. the day following I arrived at McFalls mills[89] about 60 miles where I dispatched 90 of my men Back to Render assistance on Receiving the unfortunate accounts of Col. Slyngsbees misfortune, but it was too late as the Rebels had taken to the woods and got off. I here had information of the Rebel Col[n] Wade[90] with 450 militia was then on his march to attack Col[n] M[c]Neal[91] who had assembled 70 of the Loyal Militia of Bladen and then lay on the side of Downing Creek. I

tions of Loyalists," pp. 208–9. Clark, *State Records*, XV, 595; XIX, 672. Sabine, *Loyalist Sketches*, II, 543.

[88] JOHN SLINGSBY, a merchant of Wilmington, owned the firm of John Slingsby and Company with stores at Cross Creek and Wilmington. He reluctantly signed the Continental Association and in October, 1775, briefly was a member of the Committee of Safety. When Wilmington was occupied by the British he was appointed a colonel in the Loyal Militia. With Colonels Ray and McNeill he led the raid on Cross Creek on August 14 and commanded the post at Elizabethtown. Fanning appears to be unaware of the surprise attack by the Bladen County militia led by Lieutenant Colonel Thomas Brown. The date of this skirmish is not definitely known but appears to have been August 27, 1781. McEachern and Williams, *Safety Committee Minutes*, pp. 4–5, 21, 24, 58–60, 64, 132. Clark, *State Records*, XXII, v, 566, 1047. Demond, *Loyalists*, pp. 144–45. Caruthers, *Revolutionary Incidents*, pp. 397–419. Sabine, *Loyalist Sketches*, II, 309–10.

[89] McPhaul's Mill (usually McFall's in early accounts) on Drowning Creek in Raft Swamp was an important Loyalist rendezvous. It was owned by John McPhaul and was mentioned as early as 1770. The site is located in present Hoke County southwest of Raeford. Drowning Creek is a major tributary of the Lumber River and forms the southern boundary of Moore County. Raft Swamp flows into present Robeson County and the Lumber River. Clark, *State Records*, XV, 590; XXII, 546, 549.

[90] THOMAS WADE (d. 1786), a planter and tavern keeper, was in Anson County by 1770. Before the Revolution he was a justice of the peace and was appointed to the provincial congress in December, 1776. He attended the third and fifth provincial congresses in 1775 and 1776. Appointed a colonel of minutemen in September, 1775, Wade was named colonel of the Anson County militia on March 2, 1776, and held this position throughout the war. He served as a state senator in three sessions of the General Assembly, 1780, 1782, and 1783. Saunders, *Colonial Records*, IX, 1033; X, 127, 204, 472. Clark, *State Records*, XIV, 750–52; XV, 526; XVIII, 4; XXIII, 972. Cheney, *North Carolina Government*, pp. 154, 157, 205, 209, 210, 217.

[91] HECTOR MCNEIL ("Old Hector") commanded the Bladen County Loyal Militia. He was a joint leader in the capture of Cross Creek on August 14 and established a post on Drowning Creek near McPhaul's Mill. His nephew Hector became the colonel of the Bladen County militia after the death of his uncle and was in Charleston in 1782. Clark, *State Records*, XV, 610; XXII, 546, 1043. Demond, *Loyalists*, pp. 220–21. Savary, *Fanning's Narrative*, p. 55*n*.

instantly dispatched an Express to Know his Situation and offering assistance, in three hours I Received for answer he would be Glad for to see me and my party, I marched directly and by day light in the morning arrived there with 155 men. our Picketts was fired upon and Retreated into Camp having exchanged several shots with those of the Rebels who, we had Information, were Crossing a Bridge on Downing Creek about 3 miles off when the Picketts fired upon them and Retreated to the Camp—who informed me that there was 420 men Crossed that Bridge: I imediately ordered all my men to arms and Counted them which in number was 225, horse and foot. I them marched immediately to attack them. when formed my little party I left Great Vacancies in order to appear as numurous as possible and to prevent their turning my flanks. we attacked them at 11 OClock and Engaged them an hour and a half where on my ordering a Charge they Retreated.[92] we pursued them 7 miles and took 54 prisoners 4 of which died that night. on our Return we found 19 Dead and the next day several Came in and surrendered all of which were wounded, and we had Reason to suppose the several died in the Swamps by the accounts we Received from those who Come in afterwards. Our loss was only 5 men wounded, one of which died, and 5 horses Killed. besides a few wounded we took 250 horses most of which were loaded with effects they had plundered from the friends of Government. and as I had formerly ordered that whoever found concealed goods of any Kind Should hold them. I also now ordered that Every man should Keep that he had taken that day. after mounting and equiping those 50 who where not mounted in the action: I then paroled the prisoners except 30 of whom I sent to wilmington under a guard of Col: McNeals men. then I with my party marched that Evening to Little River 16 miles from McFalls mill where the party Returned who had gone to Col: Slingsbys assistance, and the day following I arrived at Coxes Mill 30 miles where I issued the following Advertisement and circulated it through the County—

Advertisement—

This is to let all persons Know that do not make Ready and Repair Immediately to Camp that their property shall be seized and caused to be sold at

---

[92] The battle of Betti's Bridge on Drowning Creek, September 1, 1781, was a serious Whig defeat and a stunning victory for Fanning, leading directly to the raid on Hillsborough. Although called the battle of McPhaul's Mill by some sources, Betti's Bridge was twenty miles south of the mill. Murphey credited both sides with more troops than Fanning counts and said that the Loyalist victory was entirely due to the personal courage, coolness, and resourcefulness of Fanning. Wade's command would have been totally destroyed if McNeill had been able to follow Fanning's orders to block the only escape for the Whigs across the bridge. Hoyt, *Murphey Papers*, II, 298, 390–92.

public sale and if they are taken and brought into Camp they shall be sent to
Wilmington as prisoners and there Remain as such in the provost, and be
Considered as Rebels. also if any Rebels is willing to surrender and come in
he shall reap the Benefit of a subject

Camp: Coxes Mill   David Fanning. Col: Com^d Loyal Militia
6th of Sep^tm 1781

On the 9th of Sep^tr I was Joined by Col: McDugald of the Loyal Militia of
Cumberland County with 200 men and Col: Hector McNeal with his party
from Bladen of 70 men and in consequence of my Advertisement I had also
435 who came in and many Joined me afterwards. I had previously Determined within myself to take the Rebel Governor Burk[93] of N^o Carolina and
had a Conversation with Major Craigg on the subject; I now thought it a
favorable opportunity as I found myself at the head of 950 men of my own
Regiment Exclusive of M^cdugalds and McNeals Regiments. I acquainted
Major Rains of my Resalution, who approved of it. the Rebel General John
Butler[94] and Col: Robt Maybin[95] of the Continental army at this time lay
within 40 miles of our encampment on Cape fear River with 400 Continentals Soldiers and Butlers militia. it was supposed by my officers I intended to
attack them[.] after marching 16 miles to Rocky River[96] I went a little
Distance out of the Road to a friends house for Intelligence and situation of
the Rebels, during which time the Guide had my little army above two miles

[93] THOMAS BURKE (1747-1783), a native of Ireland, was in Orange County, North
Carolina by 1771. A delegate to the provincial congresses, he had a key role on the
committee that wrote the first state constitution and bill of rights. He was a delegate to
Continental Congress from December, 1776, to June, 1781, when he became the governor.
DAB, II, 282–83.

[94] JOHN BUTLER (d. 1786) was sheriff of Orange County in 1770. He was appointed to
the Committee of Safety for the Hillsborough District and was elected to the Fourth
Provincial Congress in 1776. By 1776 he was colonel of the county militia and the next year
he was commissioned brigadier general of his district. He commanded militia brigades at the
battle of Stono Ferry in South Carolina in 1779, the battle of Camden, and the battle of
Guilford Courthouse. In addition to his military service he served in the House of
Commons, the state senate, and on the Council of State. Ashe, *Biographical History*, I, 29–37.

[95] ROBERT MEBANE of the Hawfields section of Orange County was commissioned a
lieutenant colonel of the North Carolina continental line in November, 1776. He served in
Washington's army in the North Carolina Brigade and returned to the state with the Third
Regiment in 1779. After recuperation he was in Charleston and was taken prisoner at the
surrender in May, 1780. Exchanged after nine months imprisonment, he was acting colonel
of the militia in the summer of 1781. According to Caruthers, he was murdered in October,
1781, by a Loyalist Henry Hightower. Caruthers, *Revolutionary Incidents*, p. 361. Clark, *State
Records*, XIII, 476; XIV, 12, 70–71, 78, 80–81, 136, 292–93, 817; XV, 612; XVI, 603, 1113.
Hugh F. Rankin, *The North Carolina Continentals* (Chapel Hill, N. C.: University of North
Carolina Press, 1971), pp. 87, 166–67, 220, 232, 364.

[96] Rocky River, the major tributary of the Deep River, rises in northeastern Randolph
County and flows through Chatham County.

out of the way towards General Butler. on my Return to them I was under the necessity of making my Intentions Known, and Immediately directed my march for Hilsborough, pushed on all that day and the following night. at 7 O'Clock in the morning of the 12th we entered the Town in 3 divisions and received Several Shots from different houses. however we lost none nor suffered no damage except one man wounded: we Killed 15 of the Rebels and wounded 20. also took upwards of 200 prisoners. Amongst which was the Governor, his Councel, and part of the Continental Colonels, Several Captains and Subalterns & 71 Continental soldiers out of a Church. We proceeded to the Goal where we took 2 swivels and Released 30 Loyalists and British soldiers, one of which was for to have been hanged that day about 12 O'Clock.[97] I left Hilsborough and proceeded 18 miles that night towards Coxes Mill, in the morning I pursued my march about 8 miles further to Linleys Mill[98] on Cane Creek where General Butler and a party of Rebels had concealed themselves. Col. M[c]Neal who had the advanced Guard had neglected to take the necessary precautions for our security, & by the Information of Capt. M[c]Lain[99] from Cumberland County little River, and as soon as I discovered the situation we where in and having so great a number of prisoners. I left my station and pushed for the advanced Guard[.] on my coming up with Col. M[c]Neal I enquired the Reason of his neglect and before he could answer we were fired upon by the Rebels. they Killed 3 men amongst which was Col. M[c]Neal who Received 8 balls through him and five through his horse. I then ordered a Retreat back to where I had left the prisoners, and after securing them I made the necessary preparations to attack them which we did and after engageing them 4 hours they Retreated[.] I lost 27 men Killed and 60 so badly wounded that they could not be moved, besides 30 slightly but so that they could Keep up with our

[97] The Hillsborough raid on September 12, 1781, is considered Fanning's most daring exploit. Commanding his largest force of the war, Fanning believed that Whig resistance would collapse with a raid on the capital and the capture of the governor. Additional details of the raid are found in Governor Burke's report. Clark, *State Records*, XVI, 12–13; XXII, 102. Jesse Benton to Thomas Hart, Enoe, September 19, 1781, The Papers of Thomas J. Clay, 1737–1937, Manuscripts Division, Library of Congress, Washington, D.C.

[98] Lindley's Mill on Cane Creek in southern Alamance County (Orange County in 1781) was built by Thomas Lindley and Hugh Laughlin after August 10, 1755. It was the earliest mill in that section and is operated today as a grist mill by descendants of Lindley. Thomas Lindley, a Pennsylvania Quaker, was the father of James Lindley (see footnotes 2, 94). Orange County Deeds, I, 35–36; Register of Deeds, Hillsborough, N. C.

[99] JOHN MCLEAN of Cumberland County had a grist mill on Little River. He was a captain in the Loyal Militia and may have been at Moore's Creek Bridge. He remained in North Carolina after the war. Clark, *State Records*, XVI, 41, 591. Caruthers, *Revolutionary Incidents*, p. 196.

main body.[100] at the conclusion of the Action I Received a shot in my left arm. which broke the bone in several pieces and the loss of Blood was so Great that I was taken off my horse. and led to a secret place in the woods. I then sent Lieut. Woleston to my little army for Col. Arch^l McDugald and Major John Rains, and Lieut. Col. Arch^l McKay[101] to take the command and to send an Express to Wilmington for assistance as I was not able to take any command[.] I also desired that Major Rains should Return as soon as he could leave Col. McDugald as I thought he might be the means of saving me from the hand of my Enemies. those Gentlemen conducted themselves in Such a manner I think they deserve the applause of every Loyal Subject both for their Value and good conduct as Col. Maybin and General Butler pursued them all the way untill they meet Major Craigg coming to their assistance. they made their march good for 160 miles and never lost one prisoner but introduced Thomas Burk then Governor and his Regiment of Rebels to Major Craigg who Very well Excepted them and Major Craigg Introduced his Excellency and Regiment to the provo Master

I am informed By Letters from Col. Arch^l McDugald dated the 6th of August, 1789, that he has had no provision made for him yett, also Major Rains the 2^d of Oct^br 1789 But I am in hopes when Government Comes to be informed of the many services that they have done government they will consider them and make some allowance for them—I am personally acquainted with their servises, Major John Rains was the first man that ever took up arms with me in N. C. and the last man with me in that Country and took an Active part in Command in six and thirty scrimisges in N. C. *also Capt. Geo. Rains.*

at the departure of my little army I was left with three men and in four days 17 more came to my assistance. I made enquiery Respecting the loss of

---

[100] Generally ignored by North Carolina historians, the battle of Lindley's Mill, September 13, 1781, in terms of the numbers engaged and casualties, is one of the largest battles fought in the state during the Revolution. Fanning displayed superb tactical leadership in extricating his army and the prisoners from the initially successful ambushes by the Whigs. An excellent study by Algie I. Newlin, *The Battle of Lindley's Mill* (Burlington, N. C.: Alamance Historical Association, 1975) establishes the complexity and importance of this battle. Caruthers, *Revolutionary Incidents,* pp. 208–25. Clark, *State Records,* XVI, 244; XXII, 102. Benton to Hart, September 29, 1781.

[101] ARCHIBALD McKAY of Cumberland County was underage at the beginning of the war, but his father was banished in September, 1777. The young McKay remained on his family's property, and in March, 1781, he joined Cornwallis at Cross Creek. He was appointed a captain of the Cumberland County militia by Major Craig and was promoted to lieutenant colonel after the battle of Lindley's Mill. He went to Charleston with Major Craig and then to East Florida in the British evacuation. In 1784 he was in Nova Scotia. Loyalist Claim (North Carolina): Archibald McKay, Troxler, "Migrations of Loyalists," p. 220. Demond, *Loyalists,* p. 221.

the Rebels in the late action and found that the Inhabitants had Buried 24, and that the wounded they had left behind were 90. besides those that went off and that my party had taken 10 prisoners, in the number of the Killed was Col: Guttrell[102] and Major Knowles[103] who where Inveterate enimies to the Loyalists. the party we had Engaged I found to have consisted of 400 Continentals under the command Col: Mayben and General Butlers Militia[.] in 24 days I found myself able to *set* up and then dispatched four of my Cap^tns Hooker, Rains, Knight and Linley to Wilmington for a supply of amunition and before their return I had sent out and embodied 140 men During which time I heard of a Quantity of leather which was preparing for the use of the Rebel army and was ordered for Generals Greens Quarters at Camden. I went to the place and finding the Leather agreeable to my Information I took enough thereof for to equip the company compleatly and ordered the rest to be distroyed[.] on my Return to Brush Creek near where I had Been secreted during my illness occationed by my wounds I sent out spies for discovery. two of them Returned in less than an hour with information of 600 Rebels who were advanceing for to attack me but they proved no more than 170. these Accounts disheartined a number of my men from my being in so weak a state as they apprehended I should not be able for to command them[.] however they lifted me on my horse and I formed my men then in two Ranks and showed two fronts as they appeared both in my front and Rear. the fire continued near an hour. I lost 3 men Killed and 3 badly wounded[.] the Rebels had one Killed and several wounded then they Retreated and Rallied and attacked us again. after Retreating about a mile, which was so unexpected that I concluded they had been Reinforced. I then Retreated but without loss except my Baggage

[102] JOHN LUTTRELL of Orange and Chatham counties was one of the proprietors of the Transylvania Company that founded the future state of Kentucky. He was a captain of militia and in November, 1776, secured an appointment as a lieutenant colonel in the continental line. His continental service was spent primarily in recruiting, and in January, 1778, he resigned. In 1779 he was a justice of the peace for Chatham County and served two terms in the House of Commons in 1779 and 1781. He sought appointment as commander of the county militia in the summer of 1781 and apparently was serving in this capacity when he was killed at Lindley's Mill. Chatham County Court Minutes, February, 1775; February, 1779; Division of Archives and History, Raleigh, N. C. Saunders, *Colonial Records*, X, 256–61, 941. Clark, *State Records*, XII, 260; XIII, 5; XV, 623; XXII, 582, 585–86. Rankin, *Continentals*, p. 128. Caruthers, *Revolutionary Incidents*, pp. 216–17. Cheney, *North Carolina Government*, pp. 204, 208.

[103] JOHN NALL settled on Bear Creek in Chatham County by May, 1774, and had a grist mill and ordinary. He was appointed a justice of the peace in December, 1776. By 1778 he was a captain in the county militia and had been promoted to major by 1781. Chatham County Court Minutes, May, 1774; May, 1775; February, 1778; November, 1781; Division of Archives and History, Raleigh, N. C. Chatham County Deeds, A, 224, 230; microfilm; Division of Archives and History, Raleigh, N. C.

which they made a prize off. I then seperated *my men* into small parties untill the arrival of the 4 officers I had dispatched to Wilmington for ammunition who brought the following Letter from Major Craigg with 5000 Cartridges

Wilmington 13th of Octo^{br} 1781

Dear Sir

Your letter gave me Infinite Satisfaction from the favourable accounts it contained of your health and the probability of your soon being Restored to that Service in which you have acted so very much to your Honour. I beg you to accept yourself and convey to those of your officers whom I have not yet seen my warmest thanks for their Gallantry and good behavior. I inclose you the Commission you desired for Major Rains who I am Persuaded will endeavour to answer your warm Recommendations. I have been unfortunate enough for to lose the list of medicine you sent for. however I will desire the surgeon for to send you such as he thinks most likely to be serviceable to you, though from his not being acquainted with your case, it is all by guess.—I am much concerned to find the probability of so many of your people suffering for want of attendance or necessaries, nothing shall be wanting in my power, either in that Respect or in that of salt for their Relief. I am not at liberty to explain myself in a letter, but I hope I shall very soon *it* in my power to assist them with greater caire than at present. the moment I returned here and was informed of the Circumstances of the stallion you mention I determined it in your favour, and took him away from Mr Campbell[104] or Rather from a Gentleman *home* he had sold him to. he has been with my horses ever since and never Rode. I now send to you by Capt Linley—the long Northerly winds has prevented any arrivals from Charles town, so that we are totally without news. I wish I had got Mr Burkus paper   I am with much Regard. Your most Obt & Very faithful Servant—

J. H. Craigg.

The following is a Copy of the Letter I Received of Colonel Edmond Fanning[105] of the Kings Americans

---

[104] SAMUEL CAMPBELL was a merchant of Wilmington in the firm of Campbell and Hogg. A member of the Wilmington Safety Committee, he resigned in October, 1775. During the British occupation of Wilmington in 1781, he was a militia captain. Campbell went to Charleston with the British and became the colonel commandant of the North Carolina Loyal Militia. By May, 1783, he was in Shelburne, Nova Scotia. Loyalist Claim (North Carolina): Samuel Campbell. Troxler, "Migrations of Loyalists," p. 200. McEachern and Williams, *Safety Committee Minutes*, pp. 54, 58, 60, 123.

[105] EDMUND FANNING (1739–1818) was a native of Suffolk County, New York. He graduated from Yale in 1757 and moved to Hillsborough, North Carolina, where he was admitted to the bar in 1762. During the War of the Regulation (1768–71) he was the chief

this blank was left to Copy Letter and was not Copyed

The names of the officers of Cumberland County who acted under Col: McDugal as they was Commisoned In their different Companies who was with me at the takeing of Hilsborough

Archibald McDugald: Col.
Archibald McKay. Lieu^t Col.

The names of the officers of Bladen County who acted under Lieu^t Col. Hector McNeal as they was Commisoned in their different Companies who was with me at the takeing of Hilsborough

Hector McNeal. Lieu^t Col.
John Watson. Major.

The names of the Gentleman Officers who came as Volunteers from Wilmington for Recreation and Explore the Country and was at the taking of Hilsborough with me.

Alexander McCraw, Capt of Governor Martins Reg^t
Daniel McDanold, Lieu^t   do.   do.
Malcolm McKay. Ensign   do.   do.
John McKenzie, Capt
Hector McNeal——

antagonist of the Regulators, and in the Hillsborough riots he was mobbed and his home destroyed. Upon Governor Tryon's appointment to New York, Fanning became his private secretary and in 1774 was appointed surveyor-general of that colony. He became a Loyalist and commanded the King's American Regiment of Foot. At the end of the war he moved first to Nova Scotia where he served on the council and as lieutenant governor. He was appointed lieutenant governor of Prince Edward Island in 1786, serving until 1805. He died in London, England. He apparently was not a relative of David Fanning. *DAB*, V, 265–66.

Charles Campbell——
James Dawson

Some time after the Receipt of the foregoing Letters I entercepted an
express from Virginia bound for General Greens Camp which was at that
time near the lines not far from Charles Town amongst which was Lord
Cornwalliss Capitulation which I have since lost[.] we continued in small
parties Untill Major Craigg evacuated Wilmington[.] when one day I took a
man with me to go for Intelligence and to provide oats for the party I Kept
with me—when at a house I Spied a party of 30 Rebels coming towards the
said house where I was. we Instantly mounted and Rode off[.] on my
Return to my men I ordered 16 of them to mount and went back to the
house we had left but found them gone off[.] I pursued them about 16 miles
when we came up with them[.] Killed 3 of them and wounded 2 which I
took prisoners I had no loss or accident on our part—I had now certain Intelligence of Major Craiggs evacuating Wilmington[106] and the Rebels in
consequence of it had seperated into small parties and were Returning
towards their homes and for the space of 14 or 15 days I fell in with and
took more or less of them every day during which time I had information of
a Capt Kennedy[107] and his party who had taken a number of horses and a
quantity of household furniture[.] I followed him about 5 miles and after a
smart firing took him and 8 of his party with the Booty they had plundered[.] he gave intelligence that a Capp Lopp[108] with a party of 60 men
who had been discharged by General Rutherford were on their way home
up the country[.] the said Capt Caneday all the time of our attacking of
Lopp he stood and Looked on and as he declared that he would not make

[106] Major Craig completed the evacuation on November 18, 1781, and went to
Charleston. Fanning failed to mention the Wilmington Expedition of October and November which was organized and commanded by General Griffith Rutherford. Rutherford
raised a force of 1400 militia for the purposes of reducing Loyalist activity and forcing the
evacuation of Wilmington. Hoyt, *Murphey Papers*, II, 298–311. Ashe, *North Carolina*, I, 702.
Rankin, *Continentals*, p. 367.

[107] THOMAS KENNEDY of Silver Creek, Burke County, was a captain of militia and
commanded a company of mounted infantry in the Wilmington Expedition in October,
1781. Hoyt, *Murphey Papers*, II, 305, 308. Edward W. Phifer, Jr., *Burke: The History of a North
Carolina County, 1777–1920, With a Glimpse Beyond* (Morganton, N. C.: private, 1977), p. 309.

[108] JOHN LOPP of Rowan County purchased 265 acres on Abbott's Creek in 1764. He
was on the county Committee of Safety in October, 1775, and by July, 1781, he was a captain
in the militia. He commanded a company of mounted infantry in the Wilmington Expedition of October, 1781. By 1791 he was colonel of the county militia. Saunders, *Colonial
Records*, X, 279. Hoyt, *Murphey Papers*, II, 309. Rowan County Deeds, V, 348–49; VI, 92–93;
microfilm; Division of Archives and History, Raleigh, N. C. Delamar Transcripts: Legislative Papers Relating to Revolution Service; Division of Archives and History, Raleigh, N. C.;
LP 102, 389–90; LP 302, 748.

his escape Neither would he let any of his men if we Beat and Drove Cap[t] Lopp[.] I left him in a house with only 2 men to guard 11 of them and found them all there[.] the guard Informed me that he would not let any of his party make their escape[.] he proved so much to his honour that I gave him up one of his horses sadle and Bridle and paroled him with all his men—I at this time had but 13 men with me at a house near the Road not far from where they were to pass[.] I mounted my men and placed them in Concealment along the Road and on their coming up I ordered them to fire and then for to charge, which we did three times through them—they immediately dispersed through the woods and it being nearly dark we could not tell what Injury they suffered. on the 10th of Decemb[r] Col. Isaacs[109] came down from the mountains with a party of 300 men and formed his camp at Coxes Mill in the settlement I had formerly Ranged in—in order for to take me—where he continued near three months during which time the following proclamation was Issued—

State of N. Carolina

By the Honourable Alexander Martin.[110] Esq[r], Speaker of the Senate Cap[t] General Governor and Commander-in-chief in and over the said state.

Whereas divers of Citizens of this State have been deluded by the wicked artifices of our enimies, revolted and withdrew themselves from the faith and allegiance which before God they plighted to owe their country and treacherously to take up arms against the same being convinced that they have been betreyed by false hopes—Supported by deceit, and now find themselves deserted by our feeble and dispairing enemy and left unprotected to the vengeance of the state to inflict those punishments due to their crimes in tender compassion to the feelings of humanity to spare such who are willing to Return and stay the hand of execution in the unnecessary iffusion of the Blood of Citizens who may be Reclaimed, I have thought fit to Issue this my proclamation of pardon of such of the above

[109] ELIJAH ISAACS of Wilkes County was on the Surry County Safety Committee in September, 1775, and was named a justice of the peace in December, 1776. He became a justice of the newly formed Wilkes County in 1778, serving until 1785. A militia captain at the beginning of the war, he was promoted to major in April, 1778. By 1780 he was a colonel and was captured at Camden in August and imprisoned at St. Augustine. He was exchanged in June, 1781. Isaacs served three terms in the House of Commons from Wilkes County, 1778–80, and two terms in the state senate, 1782–83. Saunders, *Colonial Records*, X, 251. Clark, *State Records*, XII, 606; XV, 392–93; XVI, 148; XVII, 283; XXIII, 994. Cheney, *North Carolina Government*, pp. 203. 205, 207, 209, 211.

[110] ALEXANDER MARTIN (1738-1807) was born in Hunterdon County, New Jersey, graduated from Princeton (Nassau Hall) in 1756, and was in Rowan County, North Carolina by 1761. He became assistant king's attorney and an opponent of the Regulators. He

persons who may surrender themselves before the 10th Day of March next on this Express condition that they immidiately list into the Continental Batallions and there render a personal service for 12 months after the time of their Rendezous at head Quarters, and having faithfully performed the same for the said tirm it shall be deemed as having expiated their offences and be Intitled to and Restored to the priviledges of Citizens. all officers finding men of this class Guilty of Murder, Robery. and housebreaking to be precluded from the above not withstanding, and I do hereby Require the honourable the Judges of the Superiour Courts of law of Oyer and Tirminor and general Goal Delivery. and all officers Civil and military within this state to take notice of this my proclamation and Given themselves accordingly. Given under my hand and seal at arms at Halifax this 25th of Decr^m 1781. in the sixth year of our Independence

Sign^d Alexander Martin

By his Excellencys command John Hawkins

    D^y Secr^y   God save the state.——

During Col: Isaacs stay at Coxes Mill he Ravaged the whole settlement and and distroyed a number of houses belonging to the friends of Government[.] they frequently applied to me privately for advice[.] I Recommended it to them if possible to Remain Neutor and make their peace as it was at that time entirely out of my power for to protect or Releive them. a Capt Stinson[111] of this party took one of my men named David Jackson[112] an hung him up without Ceremony[.] a few Days before Col: Isaacs departure from Coxes Mill, he sent out notice for the friends of Government to meet him and he would give them protection agreeable to proclamation. but on their assembling he made them prisoners and marched them under a strong Guard to Salisbury Goal. not many days after they broke out and

attended the Third Provincial Congress, August, 1775, and was appointed lieutenant colonel of the Second Regiment. Soon promoted to colonel, he served until after the battle at Germanton October, 1777, when he resigned. He served numerous terms in the state senate from Guilford County, and because he was the speaker of the senate in 1781 he became acting governor when Governor Burke was captured by Fanning. Martin later was governor six terms, attended the Federal Constitutional Convention in Philadelphia, and was elected to the U.S. Senate 1793–99. *DAB*, VI, 333–34.

[111] Possibly JOHN STINSON who served under Major Joseph Graham in 1780–81 and was captured by the British in the action at Clapp's Mill in March, 1781. Graham records in 1820 that Stinson was living near Charlotte. Hoyt, *Murphey Papers*, I, 190; II, 284.

[112] DAVID JACKSON of Guilford County signed a Regulator petition and was a captain in command of a company of Loyalists at Moore's Creek Bridge. He was captured there but escaped by June, 1776, and was in Chatham County. The provincial congress raised a unit of light horse to apprehend Jackson and other Loyalists in the fall of 1776, and Jackson was brought to Halifax jail in December. His subsequent activities until December, 1781, are not known. Saunders, *Colonial Records*, VII, 134; X, 486, 600, 631, 664, 935–36, 940, 958.

Knocking Down the Centinels made their Escape except one who was shot in the attempt. two Captains in each county were appointed by Col: Isaacs on his leaving Coxes Mills to Keep the friends of Government down and were Going with their own men continually through the Country. during all this time I was in the woods and Kept moving with a small party as occation Required. One Evening I had assembled 30 men at a friends house and sent out Spies, they soon Returned with Accounts of a party of Rebels being within 4 miles of us and were distressing and plundering our friends[.] we Immediately set forward to Render our assistance and Got within half a mile of them. I then sent out to Get information how they were Situated and Intelligence I Received & by Break of day came upon them. we Retook 7 horses which they had carried off with a large Quantity of Baggage[.] we wounded 2 of them mortally and several slightly. we came off without Injury Except 2 horses wounded. the day following I pursued them to cumberland and in my way Burnt Capt Coxes house and his Fathers, I also had two skirmishes and Killed 2 of the Rebel party. on my Return to Little River I heard of a Capt Golson[113] who had been distressing the Loyalists and went in search of him myself, but unfortunatily I did not meet him but fell in with one of his men who had been very assiduous in assisting the Rebels. I Killed him. I mounted a man of my own on his horse and Returned back. I then took Capt Currie and the man before mentioned and went with a design of burning Capt Golsons house, which I did, and also two others in my way. I fell in with a man who had been very anxious for to have some of my men Executed. I sent him word for to moderate and he should have nothing to fear, but if he persevered I would certainly Kill him; this he took no notice of, but persisted for several months, and in observing me that day he attempted to escape from me, but I Shot him, Two days after Capt Walker joined me which made 4 of us, and hearing that one Thomson[114] a Rebel majestrate had taken up a horse belonging to one of my men I went to claim him. he gave him up without hesitation, and upon Examining him what arms he had, he owned to one Rifle, which I took from him—he also

<hr />

[113] CHARLES GOLSON (Golston) was a captain of the Chatham County militia in 1778. In 1790 he was living in Chatham County. Chatham County Court Minutes, February, 1778; Division of Archives and History, Raleigh, N. C. *1790 Census*, p. 88.

[114] JOHN THOMPSON (d. 1811) of Chatham County was a justice of the peace in 1774 and served throughout the Revolution. Thompson was on the Hillsborough District Safety Committee and in the provincial congresses in 1775 and 1776. He was elected county register of deeds in 1777 and in November, 1781, was on parole. Thompson was a delegate to the constitutional convention of 1789. Chatham County Court Minutes, February, 1775; May, 1777; Division of Archives and History, Raleigh, N. C. Saunders, *Colonial Records*, IX, 1027, 1169; X, 215. Cheney, *North Carolina Government*, pp. 155, 156, 768. Chatham County Wills, A, 161; Clerk of Superior Court, Pittsboro, N. C.

Informed me that the Rebels were willing to make peace with me on my own terms, as they would allow me any Limited Bounds I would Require, provided I would not be troublesome to them. I therefore Concluded after Consulting Capt Walker and Currie to demand the following terms which I forwarded by a prisoner I had taken, and in order to convince them that my Intentions were Sincere I Released him for that purpose though he had been a means of murdering several.

Terms Required by Col: David Fanning from Governor Burke forwarded to him by Lawyer Williams[115] and Capt Ramsay[116] 1st Batt^n N. Carolina Continentals——1st that every friend of Government shall be allowed to Return to their Respective homes unmolested—2^d that they shall be under no Restriction of doing or causing to be done anything prejuditial to the interest of his majesties Government. 3rd that they shall not be under any obligation to act in any public station or even to take up arms or be compelled to do any thing injurious to his Majestys good Government. 4th that they shall not pay or Cause to be paid any taxes or money so levied by your laws during the continuance of the present War to support your army their Industry.

If these terms are granted I Request they may be Immediately conveyed to me at my Quarters by a flag of truce appointed for that purpose and by such officers as I can Rely on from under your hands and seals. if these terms are not granted you may Depend upon my Sword being continually unsheathed, as I am determined I will not leave one of your old offenders alive that has Injuried his majesties Government and friends, who would have been of Service to your country in a future day, and I do hereby Recommend it to you to Govern your selves accordingly.

January 7th 1782   David Fanning Col:
To Mr James Williams   Joseph Currie
and Capt Matth: Ramsey   Stephen Walker   Cap^ts

---

[115] JAMES WILLIAMS of Chatham County qualified as an attorney at the county court in May, 1777, and in Cumberland County in October. In February, 1778, he was named the state's attorney for Chatham County. He became a justice of the peace and was on parole in November, 1781. Chatham County Court Minutes, May, 1777; February, 1778; November, 1781. Cumberland County Court Minutes, October, 1777; Division of Archives and History, Raleigh, N. C.

[116] MATTHEW RAMSEY lived on Rocky River in Chatham County and was appointed in November, 1776, a militia captain and a captain in the Ninth Continental Regiment. Captured by Fanning in the Chatham County Courthouse raid in July, 1781, he was later exchanged. Ramsey served in the House of Commons in 1782. Saunders, *Colonial Records*, X, 944, 949. Clark, *State Records*, XIV, 543–45; XVI, 235–36; XXII, 551. Cheney, *North Carolina Government*, p. 209. Chatham County Deeds, B, 131; C, 373; Register of Deeds, Pittsboro, N. C.

to be forwarded by them to the Comm[r] in Chief for the time being
Hilsborough district
I Received the following Answer from Lawyer Williams

Chatham, Jan[ry] 8th 1782.
Sir——I Received Yours by Mr. Riggin[117] at the Court house on sunday last.
and immediately wrote to General Butler on the subject of your Surrender.
as mentioned in yours. his answer is that he cannot Receive you himself but
will directly write to the Governor, and as soon as he Receives his answer he
will transmitt it to Major Griffith,[118] who will send it to winsor Pearces[119] on
deep River. If I obtain liberty I will Bring it myself, in the mean time I
would Recommend a moderate conduct as the best step to bring matters to
an Accommadation. the Bearer Mr. Riggin has Executed the trust you
Reposed in him, I therefore hope you will Restore him his property—for
your Civility to me when I was a prisoner I will do any thing I can in
Honour. concerning your surrender Col: Ray[120] and Col: M[c]Dugald have
surrendered and are gone to Charles town. I am informed by Col:
Thackston[121] I am Exchanged with a number of others prisoners at Charles
town under the Cartell which is Renewed[.] you may depend as soon as I get

[117] RIGGIN cannot be identified. There was a Rigdon's Ferry on Deep River, and a
Stephen Rigdon lived in Chatham County during the Revolution. Chatham County Court
Minutes, November, 1778; February, 1779; Division of Archives and History, Raleigh, N. C.

[118] ROGER GRIFFITH (d. 1796) of Chatham County in 1774 was a constable. He became
a deputy sheriff in 1777 and was the acting sheriff in the next year. In August, 1779, he was
nominated a justice of the peace, and in 1781 and 1784 he was the county sheriff. A captain
of militia at the beginning of the war, in July, 1781, he was promoted to major. Griffith was
colonel the next year, serving until 1790. In 1785 he was in the House of Commons.
Chatham County Court Minutes, May, 1774; May, 1777; May, 1779; August, 1779;
November, 1781; Division of Archives and History, Raleigh, N. C. Clark, *State Records*, XVI,
236; XIX, 706, 855; XXI, 798, 1073. Cheney, *North Carolina Goverment*, p. 216. Chatham
County Wills, A, 80; Clerk of Superior Court, Pittsboro, N. C.

[119] WINSOR PEARCE of Randolph County was a justice of the peace from 1779 until
1785. In November, 1776, he submitted a petition to the General Assembly for property
damages by the Loyalist David Jackson (see footnote 112). Randolph County Court
Minutes, March, 1779; Division of Archives and History, Raleigh, N. C. Saunders, *Colonial
Records*, X, 936. Clark, *State Records*, XX, 64.

[120] DUNCAN RAY was colonel of the Anson County Loyal Militia. In July, 1781, he led a
raid through Cumberland County and was a joint commander of the raid on Cross Creek on
August 14. In 1782 he was in Charleston. Clark, *State Records*, XV, 589–90; XXII, 566, 1043,
1047. Demond, *Loyalists*, pp. 219–20.

[121] JAMES THACKSTON of Orange County was a militia captain in 1768 and served with
Governor Tryon in the War of the Regulation. He was appointed a colonel of minutemen in
September, 1775, and a lieutenant colonel of the Fourth Continental Regiment in April,
1776. He served in the Moore's Creek Bridge campaign, in recruiting, and with General
Lincoln in South Carolina. Captured at Charleston, he was exchanged in 1782 and retired.
He was a merchant, and in 1787 was in the House of Commons from Cumberland County.

the Governors answer you shall know it, I am
                    Sir, your most Obed^t servent
                    James Williams—
Col: David Fanning

I also Received another letter from Capt Ramsey by Another Conveyance—

                                Jan^ry 8th 1782.
Si^r   I saw a letter from you to Mr Williams and observe what you say
concerning my case as to breaking my parole that I am clear of as Major
Craigg a few days before he left Wilmington sent a party of Dragoons to
where we were paroled at the sound, and Ordered us under the main
Guard whence I made My Escape which I am certain you will not blame me
for, as you are well acquainted with my honour, when I was your prisoner I
had it in my power to escape many a time, but as long as I was trusted like a
Gentleman, or Agreeable to the Rules of War I woud Rather suffer death
than forfeit my honour. I Observe what you say concerning your parole. for
the Kind treatment I Received at your hands you may Rely on it any thing
either Mr Williams or myself can do for you in honour shall not be wanting.—Your letter I understand is transmitted to the Govr who I make no
doubt will comply with your Request. for my part I wish for nothing else but
for peace.

                                I am Sir. Your Hum^l Servt
                                Matthew Ramsey—

I lay neutril until I got further Accounts & On the 15 of January. 1782
        Mr Williams. Clark.[122] and Burns[123] was Kind Enough to wait on me at
Mr Winsor Pearces with Respect to my former proposals which I had
Requested of them with the letter as follows——

Saunders, *Colonial Records*, VII, 707; X, 205, 516. Clark, *State Records*, XI, 283–84; XVI, 543,
610; XVIII, 448, 457. Cheney, *North Carolina Government*, p. 219. Rankin, *Continentals*, pp.
192, 269, 285.

[122] ALEXANDER CLARK purchased 260 acres in Chatham County in November, 1774,
and in 1779 he received a series of state grants. He was appointed a justice of the peace in
1774 and served as a captain of light horse in the county militia. In 1778 he was elected to a
term in the House of Commons. Chatham County Deeds, A, 284; B, 329, 372, 375, 479;
Register of Deeds, Pittsboro, N. C. Saunders, *Colonial Records*, IX, 375, 1027, 1169. Clark,
State Records, XXIII, 993. Cheney, *North Carolina Government*, p. 203. Delamar Transcripts,
LP 80, 75; LP 144, 76.

[123] JOHN BURNS had land on Indian Creek and the Deep River in Chatham County. In
1775 he served as a road overseer. Chatham County Deeds, B, 263; C, 15, 189, 192; D, 377;
Register of Deeds, Pittsboro, N. C. Chatham County Court Minutes, August, 1775; Division
of Archives and History, Raleigh, N. C.

15th of Jan^en^ 1782.

Si^r^ Agreeable to your Request I have Recv^d^ Orders to offer you a parole on the terms you Desired, twenty miles East and West fifteen N. and South: Hammon Coxes mill[124] to be the centre of Your Bounds. should you encline to go to Charles town at a future Day let me Know it, and I will endeavour to get you that liberty when I see the Governor, you mention of being waylaid, you may be assured that I Know nothing of it. Mr Williams, Mr Clark and John Burns is the Gentleman that is Kind enough to wait on you with this Flagg and a Blank Parole for you to sign, and they will give you a Certificate for your Security against any of the American Troops to Remain as prisoner of War in the Bounds specified. You may Rely on it nothing Dishonourable shall be done on my part, and I have the Greatest reason to Beleive you will Act in the same Principals. No Inhabitant of this County shall be mollested either in prisoners or property who have not been guilty of Wilfull Murder, or Plundering. it is the Duty of every honest man to bring all such to Justice in Order to Restore harmony and peace once more in our Country—

I am your Ob't Hum^l^ Servt
Matthew Ramsay

To Col: David Fanning
   Per flagg

Also the following Letter was left at Mr Pearces where the three Gentleman before mentioned

Tuesday Morning

Si^r^ Agreeable to Capt Ramsays letter Left for you, we came up to Mr Pearces where we made no Doubt of seeing you, I have seen his Instructions to parole you, and You made depend no trap is meant for you to any of our Knowlege. Ray and M^c^Dugald was Received in the same manner, and no man offered to molest them. Our orders were to have Returned last night, and the light Horse under the Command of Capt Ramsay Kept Back until our Return, therefore we cannot Possible stay any longer. if you Incline to except the terms offered, which Capt Ramsay cannot alter, you will meet us at Baalam Thomsons[125] with as many of your men as you please, such as can

---

[124] HARMON COX was the son of William Cox (see footnote 56) and inherited the property from his father on the Deep River. Orange County Wills, A-53; Clerk of Superior Court, Hillsborough, N. C.

[125] BAALAM THOMPSON of Chatham County was named in March, 1775, a justice of the peace and served throughout the war. He was a captain of militia and was listed as being on parole in November, 1781. Thompson lived adjacent to the Wilcox Ironworks on the Deep

be be Received according to the terms you propose. and am y:r Ob^t Servt—

Jas. Williams

A. Clark

Jn° Burns

To Col: David Fanning

In the course of this correspondence endeavoring to make peace I had Reason to believe they did not Intend to be as good as their words, as three of their people followed Captain Linley of mine who had moved to Wotto-guar[126] and cut him to pieces with their Swords. I was immediately informed of it and Kept a look out for them; five after their Return I took two of them and hung them, *they being Deserters from the British, Col: Hamiltons Regiment,* by way of Retaliation, both on one limb of a tree, the third made his Escape. After this Col: Alston who was a Prisoner of War at this time came to me at Generals Butlers request to Know if I was willing to come to any terms, I asked the Reason Why the Governor had not answered my Letter, and what was the cause of their Beheavour to Capt Linley; I then with a number of my Officers set down and wrote the following to General Butler[127]——

Si^r   On Friday the 7th of January last I wrote to Mr Williams the terms I was willing to come under. he wrote for answer that he could not comply with my terms untill he had the Approbation of the Governor. on Wednesday the 11th Instant January—a Flagg was too meet me at Winsor Pearces with a letter, but on its Approach it was waylaid by Capt Golston with a party of men which had more the Appearance of treachery than a ——— wish for peace. had not the Gentleman (Mr Balaam Thomson) acted so Honourable. for the minute he Arrived he let me Know it, and declared himself Innocent. this Gave me Reason to think he would Act with honour still—on the fifteenth Inst. Mr Williams, Mr Clarke and Mr Burns was the 3 Gentleman that was Kind enough to weight upon me with a Blank Parole and letter from Capt Ramsay mentioned in his letter, that my Request was Granted By the Governor. in the mean time the Gentleman waiting on me at the place appointed there came round a Company from the Hawfields Commanded

River. His property was purchased for public use early in the war but later returned to him. Chatham County Court Minutes, *passim;* Division of Archives and History, Raleigh, N. C. Saunders, *Colonial Records,* IX, 1169; X, 994–95. Clark, *State Records,* XXII, 502.

[126] Watauga was a settlement on the Watauga and the Nolichucky rivers in the present state of Tennessee. It was begun in 1769 and was included in the District of Washington and the abortive state of Franklin. William S. Powell, *The North Carolina Gazetteer* (Chapel Hill, N. C.: University of North Carolina Press, 1968), pp. 519–20.

[127] See Appendix I for the original letter with Fanning's covering letter and the accompanying note by General Butler.

by a Cap[t] Scoby.[128] which plainly and Evidently appeared to me that their was nothing but Treachery meant. On Sunday the 10th of February I fell in the Rear of Cap[t] Golstons and Cap[t] Hinds and following there trail Came on them at dark. after some firing that night I rode off—and came on them next Morning. and we came upon terms of peace till I could write to their superior officers, for which I consulted with my officers and we joined with hand and heart to comply with the terms here under written——

1st   We the Subscribers do acknowledge ourselves subjects to his Brittanic Majesty as your are well ashured of our fidelity, Zeal and Loyalty to his Majestys Government, as it has Been daily the case that we have been Destroying one and others persons and property to support and uphold our oppinions, and we are hereby willing to come to a Session of arms not under Six months nor not Exceeding twelve and Condition under written——

1st   Our Request is from Cumberland twenty miles N. and S: and 30 miles E. and W. to be total Clear of your Light horse—

2[d]   Request is for every man that has been in actual arms in a pirmanent manner in order to establish a British Government, except those who have deserted from a Regular troop that has Voluntarily listed themselves, them we do obligate to deliver up, and each and Every man that are at liberty shall have a Right to withdraw themselves in the said district.

3[d]   that if any of our men should go out of the said district to plunder or distress or Murder any of the American party, that we will by Information made to me Major Rains or any of the Captains that I shall Return their names—if the Request is Granted that they Shall Immediately be apprehended and sent to any officer appointed by you to be tried by your own laws.

4th   And if any of your party shall be catched Plundering, stealing or murdering or going in private pathes with arms signifying as if they were for mischief, to be left to our pleasure to deal with as we see, cause agreeable to our laws, all publick Roads to be traveled by any person or Company unmislisted if he behaves himself as becomes an honest man, or any Army or company or waggins Keeping the publick Roads——

5th   that every person that has been in Actual Arms in manner Aforesaid, in order to Support or Establish a British Government, shall not be Interrupted of their arms, provision, person or property, if any one Residing within the said district who are subjects to the states that you should want

---

[128] ROBERT SCOBE of the Hawfields section of Orange County was in a militia company in September, 1781, under the command of Colonel Archibald Lytle. Clark, *State Records*, XXII, 101. Orange County Wills, A, 273; Clerk of Superior Court, Hillsborough, N. C.

provision or any other Article from by sending to either of the officers that I shall Appoint for that purpose or use, that we will send sufficient Guard. See them safe in and out onmislisted——

Quakers excepted from any thing whatever.

6th and that I will not in the meantime disturb nor distress any persons or persons Abiding by Your laws in the said district; all back plundering shall be Void, as it is impossible to Replace or Restore all the plunder on Either sides

7th Our Request is to have a free trade to any ports with waggons or on horse back without arms, with a pass from any Appointed Officer for Salt or any other necessaries, and we Except the two Coxes Mills to be free from any Incumberances of all Armies belonging to American

8th any of my men that has been Returned a Continental without takeing the bounty, that has been In Actual Service as abovementioned Shall Return in the Said district——

9th If our Request is Granted as Above written I Request it may be sent to me by the 8th of March, as I may forward my further determinations. if I Cannot have my Request Granted I shall exact and point out every deplausiable measures in Order to support Every person in Arms Against his Brittanic Majesty

> I am yours most Ob^t Hum^b Servt.

Given under my hand at Arms aforesaid——

David Fanning, Col: Com:g Loyal Mi.	
John Rains Major, Loyal Militia	
William Rains, Capt	Directed
John Cagle, Capt	To John
William Price Capt	Butler Gen^r
Abner Smlly Capt	of Hilsborough
Jacob Mannies Lieu^t	Destrict

Pr Favor of Col: philip Alstin

A Copy of a Letter Received from General Butler

> Mount pleasant, 5th of March. 1782

Dear Si^r/

    Your letter of the 26th of last month was handed to me last night. I have observed the Contents. had you proposed that you and the men now in Actual Service with you—would have taken a parole—to some certain bounds until You could have been sent to Charles town to be Exchanged, I could have Entered on that business, but as your propositions are many and Some of them uncustimary in like Cases I Conceive it out of my power—however his Excellency Governor Burk is now at Halifax, and I will Send

your letter with the proposals to him by Express—this is now the fifth day of March, of course it must be several days after the Eighth before his Answer can come to hand, in the mean time it may be as well to postpone the desperate Measures you have in Contemplation. I am Your Obedient
Serv[t]—
John Butler, B. G. for Hils[b] Dis[t]
P. S. if You would Choose to be confined to a Bounds any length of time it might be Continued So that you might be Sent of Immediately under an Escort of my appointing to General Greens, he has promised me to have all Such Exchanged for which I shall send to his Quarters
John Butler B. G.

About the 7th of March 1782. a Cap[t] Walker & Currie of the Loyal Militia fell in with a party of Rebels and came to an Engagement and fired for some time till the Rebels had fired all their Ammunition and then wished to come to terms of peace between each party and no plundering, Killing or Murdering should be commited on Either party or Side, which was to be concluded upon by Each Collonel for such certain Limited Bound which was to be Agreed upon by each Col[n] and if they could not agree each partys was to be neutrul untill matters was made Known Respecting the said terms they wished to agree upon, which soon after my men came to me and informed me what they had done. We Received the Rebel Col: Belfours answer that no Resting place for a Toryes foot Upon the Earth. he also Immediately sent out his party, and on the 10th the Same Company. I Seen them comeing to a certain house where we were fidling and dancing. we Immediately prepared ourselves in Readiness to Receive them. their number being 27—and our number only seven. we Immediately—mounted our horses and went some Little Distance from the house and commenced a fire for some Considerable time. night coming on they Retreated and left the Ground. Some time before while we where bereating with each other, I had Ordered and collected 25 men to have a cretain Dress made—which was Linen frocks died Black, With Red Cuffs D[o] Ellbows and sholders cape also, and Belted with Scarlet, which was a total Disguise to the Rebels which the red was all fringed with Large white fringe and on the 12th of March[129] my

---

[129] Fanning's chronology here is off a day. The Randolph County "scourge" was on March 11–12, 1781. There are various dates given for the death of Colonel Balfour, but the most acceptable is March 11. Whig sources corroborate Fanning's account. Major Absalom Tatom reported that Captain Bryan and a Mr. King were killed on the same day with Balfour, and Colonel Collier's house as well as two others were burned. Unreported by Fanning was the physical assault on Balfour's sister Margaret and his daughter Tibby (see footnote 60). Clark, *State Records*, XVI, 244–45. Caruthers, *Revolutionary Incidents*, pp. 322–25.

men being all Properly Equipped assembled together in order to give them a small scorge which we set out for, one Belfours plantation where we came upon him, he endeavored to make his Escape, but we soon prevented him, having Fired at him and wounded him, the first ball he Received was through one of his Arms, and Ranged through his body, and the other through his neck, which put an end to his commiting any more ill Deeds, also wounded an other of his men. then proceeded on to their Col^n Collier belonging to the said county of Randolp and on our way we burnt several Rebel Houses, and catched several prisoners, the night coming on and the distance to the Said Collonels was so far it was late before we left there he— made his Escape having Rec^d 3 Balls through his shirt, but I took care to Distroy the whole of his plantation, I then pursued our Route and came to one Capt John Bryan^s[130] and Other Rebel officer, which I told him if he would come out of the house I would Give him a parole, which he Refused saying that he had taken a parole from Lord Cornwallis swearing by God he had Broke that and said he would also Break our Tory Paroles, with that I Immediately ordered the house to be Set on fire, which was instantly done, and as soon as he see the flames of the fire encreasing he called Out to me and desired me to spare his *house* for his wife and Childrens sake and he would walk out with his arms in his hands. I immediately answered him that if he would walk out that his house and property should be saved for his wife and children. which he came out, and when he came out he Said here Damn you, here I am, with that he Received two Balls, the one through his head and the other through his Body—he came out with his Gun *cocked* and sword at the same time—the next day following being the 13th March was their Election day to appoint Assembly men and was to meet at Randolph Court house, which I proceeded on in Order to see the Gentleman Representatives. their Geting entelligence of my coming they Immediately Scattered which I prevented their doing any thing that day——
from thence I pursued on to one Major Dugins[131]—House or Plantation and Distroyed all his property, and all the Rebel Officers property in the settlement for the distance of 40 miles, on our way I Ketched a Commis-

[130] JOHN BRYANT of Randolph County was captain of the county militia and served as a deputy sheriff in 1779 and 1780. Randolph County Court Minutes, March, 1779; March, 1780; December, 1782; Division of Archives and History, Raleigh, N. C.

[131] THOMAS DOUGAN (d. 1795) purchased 520 acres in Rowan County on the Deep River in 1763. When Randolph County was formed in 1779, he was a captain of the militia and was promoted to major the next year. Dougan served in the state senate in 1783, 1784, and 1788 and was a delegate to the constitutional convention of 1788. Rowan County Deeds, V, 393–94; microfilm; Division of Archives and History, Raleigh, N. C. Chatham County Court Minutes, June, 1780; Division of Archives and History, Raleigh, N. C. Hoyt, *Murphey, Papers*, II, 392–93. Cheney, *North Carolina Government*, pp. 211, 212, 215, 221, 767.

sary[132] from Salisbury who had some of my men prisoners and almost perished them and wanted to hang Some of them, which I carried him Immediately to a certain tree where they had hung one of my men by the name of Jackson, and I delivered him up to some of my men who had been treated ill when prisoners and they Immediately hung him. After hanging 15 minutes cut him down, in the mean time their was about 300 Rebels had embodied and came after us, which from the Rainy Weather our Guns would not fire on either Side. we were oblidged to Retreat on Account of their Numbers being so much Superior. We had Received no Damage. About the 8th of April a certain Capt Williams came into the Settlement and sent an old woman to me to inform me that he had arrived from Governor Burks that Instant, and had come in order to see me, which by her Descriptions I and my Little party Immediately met him and he informed me that he had come to Know If I was willing to come upon those terms I had already presented and requested to have from under my own hand a true Copy of it, and that Governor Burk would do Every thing in his power to have the same agreed upon by his Council and Assembly, for which purpose the Said Williams was sent from the Governor. he also tould me that the Governor had said that any thing I should do or cause to be done from the Character he had heard from the British in Charles Town that he had not the least doubt but what they would assent to any proceedings I should undertake to do and also whished to make a peace with me, Saying if I was taken prisoner and Killed that 100 would certainly loose their lives for it, and lookt upon much Better to come upon terms of peace, and that he had heard when in Charles town that I was Killed, which occationed him to Runaway from Charles town, upon which I gave him a Copy of the Articles which I wished to Comply to with.

which he ordered all the Light horse to Depart from their Different Stations till they had received Orders from the Governor an Council. as I was also Oblidged to lay neutrell untill—receiving their answer, which was to be upon terms of honour between Both Sides. with which the Different Capts Commanding the Rebel Light Horse wrote to me respecting the same—which appears by the following Letters——

Sir   I Received a few Lines this day from Capt Edward Williams[133] informing me that you and he had come Down yesterday. signified to me that

---

[132] Archibald Murphey identifies the executed man as Daniel Clifton. A DANIEL CLIFTON served as a sergeant in the Tenth Continental Regiment from June, 1779, for eighteen months. Hoyt, *Murphey Papers*, II, 398. Clark, *State Records*, XVI, 1035.

[133] EDWARD WILLIAMS of Richmond County was in the House of Commons five terms between 1781 and 1790 and was a delegate to the constitutional conventions in 1788 and

you and himself are upon terms of Compromising Matters on Condition that I will stop the County Light Horse from pursuing you) you may rest ashured it is my Desire to be at peace with all Men. Capt Riddle and his company is at the court house. I have ordered him to stand there untill further orders. and will send after Capt Goldston and desire him in also. I shall set off this morning to the Assembly, and if it is in my power to do or cause any thing to be done that shall cause peace and harmony over Land, you rest ashured I will do my best and Second Capt Williams, tho he give no account of your proposals, and am with Respect Yours

Hum^bl Ser^vt

April 9th 1782.   Signed   Roger Griffith, Major
To Col: David Fanning

Camp at Mr Carrs. Ap^rl 10th 1782

Si^r   I Receiv^d Orders from Major Griffith concerning some terms between him and you and shall withdraw my men and Capt Golstons as we are both together, and will not proceed any further after apprehending you. nor yours unless you come into our County Doing Mischief. untill further orders from, Your Hum^bl Servt

Signed   Joseph Russur[133a]

To Col: David Fanning

Hoping you nor yours will not Interrupt any of the Inhabitants of Chatham untill Matters are further Settled.

William Golston.

Si^r   I Received your Letter which Gives me great Satisfaction to hear that you and Some of the Officers has come upon terms of peace, which is all I would Crave, but I Should be glad that for one of the Officers in Company should meet you and have some Conversation together, and be upon honour, and if we can come upon terms agreeable to both I Should Immediately march my Company home. So I will be at Mr Mullins this Evening at two O'Clock and if you will meet and Converse across the River or any other place you will Choose

April 12th 1782   I am Si^r Your Ob^t
          Signed   Thomas Dougan, Capt of Light horse.
Col: David Fanning

1789. He was county sheriff in 1784. Cheney, *North Carolina Government*, pp. 208, 210, 221, 223, 226. Clark, *State Records*, XXI, 1077.

[133a] JOSEPH ROSSER settled on Bear Creek in Chatham County and served as a tax collector, constable, and militia captain during the Revolution. He resigned as major of the militia in 1790. Chatham County Court Minutes, November, 1777; May, 1778; Division of

April 17th 1782

Si^r)   I as an Officer in behalf of the States of North Carolina have turned out in order to suppress any persons disturbing the peace of Said States, but when Arrived to Deep River I understood that you and Capt Williams and Dugan was about to make a treaty of peace for Some time (which I approved of Very well) and withdrew my Troop towards Home, but to my Surprise on my way I understood that your men was a Robbing of the Peaceable and inoffensive people of Cane Creek and Rocky River, which wicked conduct and the Great Desire I had for the wellfare of My Country Introduced me for to stay a little Longer and Endeavour to stopp such Robbery. I therefore wish to inform you that I did not pretend with any view of making you any way dishonourable, but many persons not owing a true allegiance to the Laws of this State are running at large and Call you their Officers. as I hope you are a Gentleman and will not protect any Vagabond I would thank you to let me know Every particular of your Treaty, or what Bounds you have, and upon the Honour of a Gentleman I will not Interrupt any person within Said Bounds, that is of good Character with you. I would recommend that you would order Joseph Currie and Blair[134] to Return the Widow Dixons[135] property which they Robbed her of, and I will not write to the Governor concerning of it. as you want peace he would think very little of your honour if he heard that your men was Robbing his people after you Petitioned to him.

Si^r I am in Behalf of the States
Signed   Edward Guin.[136] Capt

Col: David Fanning

About 18th of Apr^l the aforementioned Capt Williams came to me again at Fork Creek and gave me the following Inteligence, and informed me that the originals Articles of Treaty had been laid before the Governor and Assembly and was upon a Conclusion of granting me the terms I wanted,

---

Archives and History, Raleigh, N. C. Clark, *State Records*, XVI, 210–12; XXI, 802. Chatham County Deeds, B, 415; D, 428, 634; Register of Deeds, Pittsboro, N. C.

[134] THOMAS BLAIR was a Loyalist militia captain and was seriously wounded at Pyle's Massacre (see footnote 51). To escape the war he went to Grayson County, Virginia, and eventually built an ironworks on Chestnut Creek. Later he was involved in partnerships in two other ironworks or furnaces. Wynne, *Fanning's Narrative*, p. 77n. "Thomas Blair, A Tory Captain," *The North Carolina Genealogical Society Journal*, III (August, 1977), 165.

[135] ELIZABETH ALLEN DIXON was the widow of Quaker Simon Dixon, who had built Dixon's Mill on Cane Creek (see footnote 54).

[136] EDWARD GWIN lived on the Haw River in Orange County. He was an ensign in August, 1776, in the county militia and participated in the Cherokee campaign. Orange County Deeds, II, 162; IV, 544; IX, 75; Register of Deeds, Hillsborough, N. C. Saunders, *Colonial Records*, X, 753.

but was prevented by a Col: who came from over the mountains, and was one of the Assembly who did every thing agamst it, their exceptions was that the articles respecting the Continental Soldiers to be taken of, and also that they could not think of allowing any passports for any of the friends of Government to have any correspondence or Connections with the British, every other article they were willing to Grant. their Assembly Continued on the Business for three Days, as Mr Williams Informed me. my answer was that I would forfeit my life before I would withdraw any one of the Articles that I had presented.—as I still wish to hold the same Connection with the British as formerly. I likewise tould him that I understood that they had picked out 24 of their best horses and men from Virginia in order to pursue me; and my Answer was to Mr Williams that they might do their best and be Damned as I was fully Determined to still Support my Integrity, and to exert myself in the Behalf of the King and Country more *sincere* than ever I did. with this Mr Williams Departed.

I then Set out for Chatham to where I heard of a weding that was to be that day, on my way I took one prisoner. before I Came to the House, there being but 5 of us we Immediately Sorounded the House in full Charge. I ordered them Immediately out of the House, which 3 of my men went into the House, and Drove them all out one by one and Caused them all to stant in a Row to Examine them, to see if I Knew any of them that was bad men; with which I found one by the name of William Doudy[137] Concealed up stairs, one of my men fired at him as he was Running from one house to the other, he Received the Ball in his shoulder. I then having my pistols in my hand I Discharged them both at his Breast, with which he fell and that night Expired. I then paroled the rest on the 25th

I concluded within myself that it was Better for me to try and settle myself being weary of the disagreeable mode of Living I had Bourne with for some Considerable time.

And for the many Kindnesses and the Civility of a gentleman who lived in the Settlement of Deep River had Introduced me to pay my addresses to his daughter, a young Lady[138] of 16 years of age; the day of marriage being appointed on makeing it Known to my people Capt William Hooker and Capt William Carr agreed to be married with me—they both left me to make

---

[137] WILLIAM DOWDY of Chatham County in the period 1775–78 is mentioned in the court minutes as a juror and road overseer. Chatham County Court Minutes, November, 1775; August, 1778; November, 1778; Division of Archives and History, Raleigh, N. C.

[138] SARAH CARR (1766-1833) was born in Virginia and met Fanning in Chatham County, North Carolina, where they married in late April, 1782. William Carr was apparently her brother. The Fannings had one daughter, Ferebee, and two sons, Ross Currie Carr (1791-1871) and David William (1793-1810). Howe, *"Fanning,"* 1, 15, 16.

themselves—and the Supposed wives Ready. and the Day before we was to be coupled, the Rebels before mentioned with those Good horses came upon them and Capt Hookers *his* horse being tied so fast he could not get him loose untill they catched him and murdered him on the spot, myself and Capt Carr was married and Kept two Days meriment. the Rebels thought they was shure of me then, however I took my wife and concealed her in the woods with Capt Carrs, and caused a anonoration to be put out, that I was gone to Charleston. in order to be convinced the Rebels sent a man in as a Spye with 2 letters from General Laslie,[139] with Instructions to me to inlist men for the Service which I Knew was forged—in order to betray me, and from the person or Commanding officer of the Rebel light Horse Sent me the following Letters, one of which I gave to General Laslie, that had his name signed to.

Charles town 20th Jan^ry, 1782

Dear Collonel.

Altho' I have not as yet the happiness of Being acquainted with you, yet I can but applause you very much for your spirited conduct and activity; the only objection I have to your conduct is your being two streneous with those who have been Subjects to his Majesty, and the Rebels have overcome and forced them to comply with their laws; if you would let them alone the Severity of the Rebels would cause them to Return to their allegiance again; but Si^r Since you have made So Brave a stand already pray stand sedfast to the End and you shall be well Rewarded at the last; try to sperit up your men and list if possible three hundred men this Spring Ready to join three hundred more which shall be put under your command, and you be Brigadier General of them and as many more as you can *git*, we shall I hope in the month of may land 1300 Troops in N. Carolina, and 300 for you to join your Corps, 1600 in the whole to act, upon theDefensive untill you are Reinforced; Keep Good Dissipline amongtess your troops and Keep out fellows who will do nothing but Plunder from amongst your people, they are but false Dependance and will not fight—but only Corrupt good men. Every man you Inlist for 12 months shall Receive 10 Guineas and a full suite of clothes. as Soon as we land our troops, and they appear under Your Command Ready for action. I can assure tis your fame and worthy actions has throug and by Major Craigg has given—*has* Reached his Majestys Ears

---

[139] ALEXANDER LESLIE (1730-1794) was a career soldier and had become a lieutenant colonel by 1766. He was a brigadier general in 1776 at the battle of Long Island and served under Cornwallis in the campaign in the Southern colonies. He had an important role in the battle of Guilford Courthouse and at the end of the war was the commander at Charleston. Benjamin F. Stevens (ed.), *The Campaign in Virginia 1781. An Exact Reprint of Six Rare Pamphlets on the Clinton-Cornwallis Controversy* (London: private, 1888), p. 442n.

and I expect perhaps by the next packet Boat you will get a genteel present from our Most Gracious Soverign, so hoping you will be the way of your Duty I will take my leave of you without mentioning your name or Subscribing mine least this might miscarry: the man who is Intrusted with the care of this *dare* not at present be seen in it. But a friend and Send it to the man it is— Directed To——

> I am Dear Si^r Your
> Ob^t Hum^bl Servt

To Col: Fanning in
   North Carolina

A letter from the Traitor who Brought those two letters from General Laslie:—

Dear Si^r I would come to see you myself but am affraid of the Rebel light Horse. I have a Great many things to acquaint you with and good deal of good news, but dares not wright it for fear of miscarriages; if you have any Desire of Seeing me you must come soon, nay instantly. Dont let the bearer Know the contents of the letters, the fewer are trusted the better, in the meantime, I am your friend and Hum^bl Ser^vt

> Joseph Wilson

To Col: Fanning, April 29th 1782

My answer was in Major Rains name as follows
> 31st of April 1782

Si^r   I am very sorry to think that there is so many Damned foolish Rebels in the world as to think Col: Fanning should even be Deceived by such Damned infernal writings *as* I have received from you, Col: Fanning is gone to Charles town and is not to Return here untill he comes with forces Sufficient to Defend this part of the Country, and I would have you to disband and be gone Immediately for if ever I hear of any of your people comeing with any thing of the sort I will come and Kill him myself. I am in Behalf of his Majesties Armies

> John Rains,
> Maj^r L. Militia

To
Joseph Wilson

On the 1st of May 1782 I heard a waggon Going on the Road as I Emmagined She was going Down to market. as I heard of a number of waggons which was to proceed Down with Liquors to market on the 2^d I mounted and pursued the wagon which I heard the day before, and as I was about Setting out for Charlestown I concluded to have a frolic with my old friends before we parted. when after Riding about 11 miles I overtook the Said wagon which waggon belonged to a certain man who had been taken prisoner and paroled by the British and had broke his parole. In the meantime I was examining his papers I Set a Centinel over him, he Knowing himself guilty expected nothing but Death. which he took an opportunity and spring upon my own Riding mare and went off with my saddle, holsters pistols and all my papers of any Consequence to me—also we fired two guns at him, he Received 2 Balls through his Body but It did not prevent him from siting the Saddle and made his Escape, I took the other man and Caused him to take me to this man's plantation where I took his wife and three negro boys and 8 head of horses and took his [wife] and Keep her in the woods for 3 Days and sent the other man to see if he would deliver my papers, for which he wrote me the following answer or Letter—

Si[r] Col. Fanning I hope you do not blame me for what I did hoping you will have mercy on me as I am wounded and let my wife come to me, your mare shall be Returned to you without fail, your mare I don't Crave and I am in hopes You dont Covet mine, I beg that you would have pity on my wife and Childrens, Negroes and horses, I am willing you shall Keep till you get your mare. I have Sent to a Doctor, but the mare will be back tonight, no more but you may Depend on my word

To   Signed   Andrew Hunter[140]
Col. David Fanning

I also Received the following Letter from Edward Williams in favor of the Subject of the Mare

Si[r] These few lines comes to let you Know that I have this day Seen Mr. Hunter, and he is Badly wounded and desires you would let his wife come to him Immediately, and as to the rest of his property you are welcome to Keep untill Such times you get your mare returned which shall be as soon as possible, and as she is gone at this time after the Doctor, But she shall be returned to you with all Speed, as Soon as She Returns M[r] Hunter is also very ill.

                I am Yours Obedient
                Humb[l] Serv[t]

Col David Fanning   Edward Williams

[140] The escape of ANDREW HUNTER of Randolph County on Fanning's famous mare "Red Doe" or "Bay Doe" is one of the best known incidents in the folklore of the Revolution. Fanning's strenuous effort to recover the horse is an indication of the high value he placed on her. Hunter later moved to South Carolina. Caruthers, *Revolutionary Incidents*, pp.

On the 7th of may finding I could see no opportunity of geting my mare, notwithstanding she was one of my prinsople Creatures and a mare that I set great store By. I gave 110 Guineaes for her. I was obliged to turn loose all his horses Except one, as they was of no account to me in the situation I was in, the negroes I Kept. I then proceeded on to Major Gainnors truce land[141] on Peedee in South Carolina where he had made a Truse with the Rebels for some time before and I continued there untill June when I left my wife, horses and negroes and then as I was Entirely a stranger to the Situation of the country and Roads I was obliged to procure a pilot to proceed to Charleston which I could not get one for less that 20 Guineaus. after my Departure I fell in with the Rebel Dragoons commanded by Col. Baillie[141a] from Virginia. I was with them for about an hour, and informed them that we was Some of the Rebel party then on our way to General Marions[142] Quarters, which they never Discovered as otherways than as such. it being Dusk of the evening we fell in the Rear and went into the woods and struck our camp and promised them we would see them the next morning. However we proceeded on that night and arrived at Herralds point on the 17th of June and Immediately Procured a passage to Charles town where I immediately applied for a Flagg to send after Mrs Fanning and property, the flagg had left Charles Town 2 days when she came in as Major Gainer had applied to General Maron for a pass for her to proceed to Charles town But would not let her have any of our property or even a Negro to wait on her.

Here ends the Jonas Howe transcript of Fanning's Journal. *The following portion is from pages 36 to 51 of the Alfred W. Savary edition. With the exception of the documents relating to Fanning's claim for property losses and his military service, the Wynne edition omitted this material.*

273–81. Hoyt, *Murphey Papers*, II, 398–400. Alexander Gregg, *History of the Old Cheraws* (New York: Richardson and Co., 1867), pp. 396–97.

[141a] See page 114.

[141] Major Micajah Gainey and Francis Marion established by truce a neutral area between the Pee Dee River and the North Carolina border in 1781–82. Fanning was specifically exluded from the agreement. The area increasingly became a refuge for North Carolina Loyalists raiding across the border. Hoyt, *Murphey Papers*, II, 309–10. Gregg, *Cheraws*, pp. 374–76. Hugh F. Rankin, *Francis Marion: The Swamp Fox* (New York: Thomas Y. Crowell Co., 1973), p. 282.

[142] FRANCIS MARION (1732-1795), the "Swamp Fox," was a delegate to the provincial congress of 1775 and became a captain in the Second Regiment of South Carolina Continentals. At Savannah in 1779 he was serving as lieutenant colonel in command of the regiment. By 1781 he had been appointed a brigadier general of militia and achieved his greatest fame as a Whig partisan. In June, 1782, Fanning vowed to the British command in Charleston that he would take Marion dead or alive. *DAB*, VI, 283–84. Rankin, *Marion*, p. 283.

In a short time loyalists that had got into Charleston from different parts of the world, hearing that the Southern Colonies were to be evacuated by the British forces, called a meeting to point out some measures to try to hold some foothold in the country, until we had got some part payment for our property which we were obliged to leave if we left the country. Hand-bills were struck and stuck up through the town for the loyalists to choose their representatives to represent our situation and the desire we had to support ourselves and property. It was proposed that twenty-five gentle-men should be chosen a committee for that purpose. The days were appointed to take votes. I was chosen amongst others; and drew up a petition and sent to Sir Guy Carleton,[143] Commander-in-Chief, praying the liberty of keeping the town and artillery, as they stood on the works, and despatched two gentlemen off with our petition; our request was not granted. I have hereunto set forth the names of the gentlemen representatives:

Col. Ballingall, Jas. Johnston, Esq.; Robert Williams, Esq.; Lt.-Col. Dupont, Col. Robt. Wm. Powell, Col. Gray, John Gailliard, Esq.; Col. Cassels, John Rose, Col Pearson, Maj. Wm. Greenwood, Col. Philips, Maj. Gabriel Capers, Col. Hamilton, Lt.-Col. Thos. Inglis, Wm. Carson, John Hopton, Esq.; Dr. Wm. Charles Wells, Robt. Johnston, Esq.; Col. Thomas Edgehill, John Champniss, Andrew Millar, Esq.; Col. Samuel Bryan, Col. David Fanning, Doctor Baron.

I remained in Charleston until the 5th of September, and my horses having got recruited, and one of my negroes having made his way good through the country, came down to me; I then set out for the country again, on account of my misfortune of losing my mare, which was of great value to me. I went up to the settlement again, to the man I sent to Hunter before, and he informed me that Hunter refused five negroes for the mare and would not return her. He also went to where I left one of the negroes and took him and sent him over the mountains to keep him out of my way. I continued about in the settlement until the 22nd of the month, trying to get her, but was disappointed in my hopes. Knowing that Charleston was to be evacuated, I was obliged to return; and as I was on my way, I understood my mare was at a certain place, about 125 miles from Charleston, being about

---

[143] GUY CARLETON (1724-1808) entered the army in 1742, served in the French and Indian War, and was promoted to colonel by 1762. He was appointed lieutenant governor of the province of Quebec in 1766 and the next year became acting governor. He left his post in 1770 but in 1775 was reappointed governor of Quebec and was commander of forces in Canada. Promoted to lieutenant general in 1777, he was eventually named the commander-in-chief in America, succeeding Sir Henry Clinton. After the war he served again as governor of Quebec and then in 1791 became governor of lower Canada. *DNB*, III, 1002–4.

half the distance from where I then was toward Charleston. I instantly pursued on my journey to the place where she then was. I came within a mile of where I heard she was, and my riding horse was so particularly known, I sent a man up to the house and he was known, and they directed us the wrong way, and immediately sent word to where my mare was. I found out we were wrong; and took through the woods and to a house within a half a mile, where they had word of my coming and were making ready to go to their assistance, but seeing us come up, he immediately left his horse, and was running off through a field, and turned round and presented his piece and snapped, but she missed fire; with this, I ordered one of my men to fire at him, who shot him through the body, and despatched his presence from this world. The other two men that was at the house that did not run, informed me that they had received word of my coming a half an hour before I arrived, and also that there were men lying in ambush ready to attack me. With this, the man who had my mare went off with her, and having only two men and my negro that set out with me from Charleston, also two little negroes that I had for my mare, I thought it was my best way to proceed to Charleston, and on the 28th September I arrived at Charleston, where the shipping was ready for me to embark for St. Augustine.

The following is a Proclamation which I got when I was out in the country, nailed to Coxe's Mill:

State of North Carolina:

By his Excellency Alexander Martin, Esq., Governor, Captain-General and Commander-in-Chief in and over the said State.

A PROCLAMATION

Whereas divers citizens of this State have withdrawn themselves from their allegiance and joined the enemy of this and the United States, seduced by their wicked artifices, now find their hopes, supported by deceit, totally blasted and left unprotected to the Justice of their country ready to inflict those just punishments due to their crimes. But in compassion to such who are truly penitent and to stop the further effusion of the blood of citizens who may be reclaimed, by and with the advice and consent of the Council of State I have thought proper to issue this my proclamation of pardon to all such of the above persons who shall within ten days after the date hereof surrender themselves to any commanding officer of any troops of the State or any of the United States acting in conjunction with the same, on this express condition that they renew the oath of allegiance and enter into one of the Continental battalions of this State and there serve twelve months after the time of their rendezvous, which service being faithfully performed shall expiate their offences and entitle them to the restoration of their property and every other privilege of a citizen, precluding all those guilty of murder, robbing, house-breaking and crimes not justifiable by the laws of war from the above pardon, notwithstanding notifying all such persons that unless they surrender at the time aforesaid, those taken prisoners shall be deemed prisoners of war, and liable to exchange except as above provided. The enemy will exchange the same, otherwise they shall be subjected to the penalties of the said law which will be inflicted upon them.

By Order of his Excellency Alexander Martin, Esq.,

Bennett Crofton, Major, States Legion.

June the 15th, 1782.

During my absence from Charleston, the loyalists were signing to go under my directions to East Florida, and as soon as I came to town I ordered them all to get on board, and on the 6th of November I went on board the transport ship, the *New Blessing*, commanded by Thomas Craven, where I continued on board the said transport for eight days before she set out for St. Augustine. Arrived the 17th said month, where we came to anchor, and there laid eight days more; at the expiration of that time I went on shore and three days after had my property landed, about twenty-seven miles distance from St. Augustine, upon the Matanzeys,[144] where I had some thought of settling. I continued there for some time and from thence proceeded to Halifax River, being about fifty-five miles from St. Augustine. There I undertook to settle myself and to make a crop, thinking to begin the world anew, being tolerably well provided for with negroes.

In the last of February I met Major Andrew Deavoce,[145] who was beating up for volunteers to go to take New Providence. I also agreed to join him and took a copy of the Articles and went home and raised thirty young men for that expedition, and had them in readiness to embark and waited for Major Deavoce arrival at the inlet of Halifax, until I heard he was gone. A true copy of the original is hereunto set forth:

Articles of Agreement between Major Deavoce and the Volunteers, for an expedition immediately against New Providence:

[144] Matanzas Inlet is about twenty miles south of St. Augustine.

[145] ANDREW DEVEAUX, a native of Beaufort, South Carolina, joined General Augustine Prevost in 1778 and was at the siege of Charleston in 1780. He raised a unit of Royal Foresters (scouts) and served as a major in the Granville County Loyal Militia. He planned and led the expedition from East Florida in April, 1783, that captured the island of New Providence, Bahamas, from the Spanish. Unknown in the Bahamas was the fact that the Spanish had already ceded the islands to the British by treaty. Loyalist Claim (South Carolina): Andrew Deveaux, LVIII, 32–39. Siebert, *Loyalists in East Forida*, I, 145–47. Sabine, *Loyalist Sketches*, I, 377–78.

Article 1st. I do engage on my part to furnish the men with provisions, arms and ammunition for the expedition.

2nd. That the men shall be altogether under my command and not to be transferred to any other after the expedition, and that they rendezvous on the fifteenth of this month in town, and be ready to go on board on three hours' notice being given them.

3rd. That all or any of the men who shall desire to settle in that country after the reduction of it shall be provided with land.

4th. That all prizes taken by land or sea shall be equally divided among the officers and men according to their respective ranks, first deducting the expense of the expedition.

5th. That in case of mutiny or disobedience of orders the man or party concerned shall forfeit the whole of their prize money and be subject to confinement for the offence according to the nature of the crime.

6th. That a certain number of dead shares shall be reserved for the support of all wounded men, widows and orphans of men that may unfortunately fall on this expedition. Ten dead shares shall be at the disposal of Capt. Wheeler and myself for deserving men.

7th. That the person who raises the most men shall be second in command, and I do engage if any person or persons should not be willing to remain in the Bahamas to furnish them with a passage to Jamaica or back to St. Augustine.

St. Augustine, 3rd of March, 1783.

We who have subscribed our names as under, do hereby agree to go with Major Andrew Deavoce on the within expedition as volunteers, complying with the within rules and to hold ourselves in readiness for embarking on said expedition on the fifteenth of this inst. Either of us refusing to comply with the above and within rules and articles shall forfeit to Major Andrew Deavoce, his heirs or assigns, the sum of ten pounds sterling money of Great Britain.

After this I began to notice my negroes beginning to get sick and six of them died. Some time after I went to St. Augustine I was taken sick and lay at the point of death for three weeks. I then began at last to walk, and one day I went to my field to where I had a young negro about twenty years of age at work. I took my rifle with me as usual; I set her down by a tree. I felt very sick and weak; I laid myself down on some grass and my negro took up my rifle and came within ten yards and set himself down and took aim at my head, but luckily the ball missed my head about one inch, but it split my hat. I then got up and went towards him, when he ran at me with the gun and struck at my head. But I fended it off with my arms. He however broke the stock, forward of the lock. I knowing myself weak, I turned and ran sixty yards, but found myself not able to run. I got my feet entangled in some vines and unfortunately fell, and he came to me and with the barrel of my rifle he struck at me many times. I lay on my back and fended his strokes with my heels until he had knocked all the bottoms of my feet to blisters. His great eagerness to kill me put him much out of wind. I accidentally got hold of the gun barrel and he tried to bite my hand for some time. During the time of his trying to bite me, I knocked all his fore teeth out. At last he run for his hoe and made one stroke at me and broke one of the bones of my left arm. But I took the opportunity of giving him a stroke on his temple with which I brought him down. I then mended my blows until he appeared to be dead. As I had got him down my wife came in sight of me, and he lay for some time to appearance dead, until two men came to me as they had heard me hollowing. He at length come to and walked home. I confined him to take him to justice. He lived till the next day, and at the same hour the next he was sitting, eating, and all of a sudden he fell dead.

In a short time after I heard peace was proclaimed and for the loyalists to send an estimation of their losses and services; also, that the Province of East Florida was to be immediately evacuated, and the ships came to take all the provincial troops to Nova Scotia; the officers that were acquainted with me insisted for me to go with them, but I had not time to get my family and property to town in time, and as it was uncertain where I should go to, some of the gentlemen officers desired to give me a certificate to let my services be known, let me go where I would—a true copy of which is hereunto set forth:

East Florida.

We whose names are hereunto subscribed, do hereby certify that Col. David Fanning, late of the Province of No. Ca., acted in the station of Colonel of Militia of that Province, and was of the greatest service to his Majesty in suppressing the rebels during the late rebellion in North America, and that he is worthy of every loyal subject both for his valour and good conduct; that after he with his men took the town of Hillsborough, dispersed the rebel council, and took a great number of prisoners, he was on that day wounded in the left arm—that finding the town of Wilmington evacuated by the British troops, and his wound not yet well, he, for the safety of his people, divided them into small parties, and continued a long time in the back woods; that after many skirmishes in North Carolina, in the month of June, 1782, he with the utmost difficulty made his way through many interruptions of the enemy to the Province of South Carolina, where his Majesty's troops then lay; and that he was obliged to leave the province where he lived, and his property, which we are informed was considerable; and that he is now without the means of subsistence, having lost his all for and on account of his services and attachment to his Majesty's person and government.

John Hamilton,
   Lt.-Col. Com. R.N.C. Regt.
John Legett, Capt. R.N.C. Regt.
Alex. Campbell, Capt. S.C. Regt.
Geo. Dawkins, Capt. S.C. Regt.
Daniel McNeil, Capt. R.N.C. Regt.
Moses Whitley, Lieut. S.C. Regt.
St. Augustine, 20th September, 1783.

On the 25th November following, I drew up an estimate of the loss I had sustained during the late war in America, a true copy of which I hereto set forth:

Schedule of the property of Col. David Fanning, late resident of the Province of North Carolina, but now of the Province of East Florida, lost to him on account of his zeal and attachment to the British Government, and never received any part or parcel thereof, or any restoration of the same, viz:

	£ s
550 acres of land in Amelia County in the Province of Virginia, with a Virginia, with a dwelling house and other necessary buildings, a large apple and peach orchard, and large enclosed improvements	687.10
550 acres of land near said plantation, as heir to the estate of my father, and some improvement with a dwelling house	412.00
3 saddle horses	41.00
12 plantation do., three unbroke do.	96.00
2 negro slaves	100.
Debts in notes, bonds, etc.	289.
	£1,625.10

Personally appeared before me, one of his Majesty's Justices of the Peace, St. Augustine and Province of East Florida, the above-mentioned Col. David Fanning, who, being duly sworn and maketh oath on the Holy Evangelist of Almighty God, that he lost all and every part of the above-mentioned property on account of his zeal and attachment to his Majesty's cause during the late war against the revolted colonies in North America, and that he has not let, sold, bargained, bartered or disposed or impowered any person or persons to let, sell bargain, barter of dispose of any part or parcel of the same in any manner whatsoever, nor received any restitution for the same. Sworn at St. Augustine, the 25th November, 1783, before me.

John Mills, J.P.

David Fanning.

Personally appeared before me, one of his Majesty's Justices of the Peace in St. Augustine, Province of East Florida, Lieutenant Charles Robertson, Neill McInnis, and Philip Whisenhunt, refugees, of said East Florida, who being called upon by the within mentioned Col. David Fanning to value the within mentioned property, who being duly sworn, make oath upon the Holy Evangelists of Almighty God, that the within mentioned properties are well worth the sums affixed to each article, as near the value as possible if the same was to be sold, to their own knowledge and the best information they could get.

Charles Robertson.

Neil McInnis.

Philip Whisenhunt[146]

Sworn at St. Augustine, this 25th November, 1783, before me.

John Mills, J.P.

(Here follows notarial certificate by John Mills)

After my many scenes and passages through and during the late war, and often hearing the Americans had got their request, I never could put any faith in it until I saw the King's speech, of which I have hereunto set forth a true copy for the better satisfaction of those loyalists that perhaps have never seen it yet.

New York, February 9th, 1783.

By the brigantine *Peggy*, Capt. McNiel, in nineteen days from Tortola, we have received the following copy of his Majesty's most gracious speech to both houses of Parliament on Thursday, December 5th, 1782—which was brought to Tortola from Windward by Capt. Rodney, son of Lord Rodney:

My Lords and Gentlemen:

Since the close of the last session, I have employed my whole time in the care and attention which the important and critical conjuncture of public affairs required of me.

I lost no time in giving the necessary orders to prohibit the further prosecution of offensive war upon the continent of North America, adopting, as my inclination will always lead me to do with decision and effect, whatever I collect to be the sense of my Parliament and my people. I have

[146] The signatures on the original claim are Charles Robeson, Niel McInnis, and Philip Wismandt.

pointed all my views and measures as well in Europe as in North America to an entire and cordial reconciliation with those colonies.

Finding it indispensable to the attainment of this object, I did not hesitate to go the full length of the powers vested in me and offered to declare them free and independent States by an article to be inserted in the treaty of peace. Provisional articles are agreed upon to take effect whenever terms of peace shall be finally settled with the court of France. In thus admitting their separation from the crown of these kingdoms, I have sacrificed every consideration of my own to the wishes and opinion of my people. I make it my humour and ever my prayers to Almighty God that Great Britain may not feel the evils which might result from so great a dismemberment of the Empire, and that America may be free from those calamities which have formerly proved in the mother country how essential monarchy is to the enjoyment of constitutional liberty. Religion, language, interest, affections, may and I hope will yet prove a bond of permanent union between the two countries—to this neither attention nor disposition shall be wanting on my part.

While I have carefully abstained from all offensive operations against America, I have directed my whole force by land and sea against the other powers at war with as much vigour as the situation of that force at the commencement of the campaign would permit. I trust that you must have seen with pride and satisfaction the gallant defence of the Governor and garrison of Gibraltar, and my fleet after having effected the object of their destination offering battle to the combined force of France and Spain on their own coasts; those of my kingdom have remained at the same time perfectly secure, and your domestic tranquility uninterrupted. This respectable state under the blessing of God I attribute to the entire confidence which subsists between me and my people, and to the readiness which has been shewn by my subjects in my city of London and in other parts of my kingdoms to stand forth in the general defence. Some proofs have lately been given of public spirit in private men which would do honour to any age and any country—having manifested to the whole world by the most lasting examples the signal spirit and bravery of my people. I conceived it a moment not unbecoming my dignity, and thought it a regard due to the lives and fortunes of such brave and gallant subjects to shew myself ready on my part to embrace fair and honourable terms of accommodation with all the powers at war.

I have the satisfaction to acquaint you that negotiations to this effect are considerably advanced, the result of which as soon as they are brought to a conclusion shall be immediately communicated to you. I have every reason to hope and believe that I shall have it in my power in a very short time to acquaint you that they have ended in terms of pacification which I trust you will see just cause to approve. I rely, however, with perfect confidence on the wisdom of my Parliament and the spirit of my people, that if any unforeseen change in the disposition of the belligerent powers should frustrate my confident expectations, they will approve of the preparations I have thought it advisable to make, and be ready to second the most vigorous efforts in the further prosecution of the war.

Gentlemen of the House of Commons:

I have endeavoured by every measure in my power to diminish the burthens of my people. I lost no time taking the most decided measures for introducing a better economy in the expenditure of the army.

I have carried into strict execution the several reductions in my civil list expenses directed by an act of the last session. I have introduced a further reform into other departments and suppressed several sinecure places in them. I have by this means so regulated my establishments that my expense shall not in future exceed my income.

I have ordered the estimate of the civil list debt laid before you last session to be completed. The debt proving somewhat greater than could be then correctly stated and the proposed reduction not immediately taking place, I trust you will provide for deficiency, securing as before the repayment out of my annual income.

I have ordered enquiry to be made into the application of the sum voted in support of the American sufferers, and I trust you will agree with me that a due and generous attention ought to be shown to those who have relinquished their properties or professions from motives of loyalty to me and attachment to the mother country."

On the 10th of March I had some business to St. Augustine, the inhabitants of Musqueto[147] asked the favour of me to hand a petition to his Excellency the Governor, and knowing the situation of the petitioners I spoke in their behalf; asked his Excellency what answer he sent to the people, he said he should send for none of them, and if they were a mind to remove, they must get to the shipping as they could, for he said he had no vessels at that time in Government's services.

"To his Excellency Patrick Tonyn, Esq., Capt. General, Governor and Commander and Chief in and over his Majesty's province of East Florida and vice-admiral of the same: whereas your humble petitioners showeth

---

[147] The Halifax River enters the Atlantic at the present Ponce de Leon Inlet (the colonial Mosquito Inlet). Mosquito Inlet was the site of Dr. Andrew Turnbull's extensive New Smyrna colony. Siebert, *Loyalists in East Florida*, II, 325.

that they are rendered very poor and unable to remove ourselves to be in readiness to receive the opportunity offered for our removement from his Majesty's province of this East Florida which is to be evacuated; here is several poor widows as well as poor men of his Majesty's loyal subjects; we pray his Excellency would send a schooner to remove us to the vessels provided for our passage when his Excellency sees that this province will be given up; we would wish to tarry here where we have good warm houses till his Excellency sees the time draws nigh; however, we would wish to refer it to his Excellency's opinion upon the matter, and in granting of your petitioners' humble petition, your humble petitioners ever will be in duty bound to pray.

At the Musqueto, this 26th of January, 1784.

Thomas Young, Capt. S.C. Mil.

Abraham Floyd, Joseph Currie, Magee Black, Agnes Wilson, Moses Barnes, Jacob Barns, Joseph Rogers."

I left St. Augustine the 13th of said month and returned to the Musqueto and made the following speech to the inhabitants.

"**My good and worthy friends: I am now going to make some remarks as to your disagreeable situation. The distresses to which the unfortunate loyalists in America are now reduced are too poignant not to command the pity and commiseration of every friend to human nature. The man that is steeled against such a forcible impression is a monster that should be drove from the circle of cultivated society. In most situations, when calamities and misfortunes press upon our minds, hope buoys us up and keeps us from sinking into the ocean of despondency and despair, but the unfortunate loyalists have no hopes to cheer up their spirits; even this last refuge of the afflicted is denied us of enjoying peace and happiness which our fore-fathers and ourselves were born under. During a seven years' war we have been induced to brave every danger and difficulty in support of the Government under which we were born, in hopes that we and our children would reap the fruits of our labour in peace and serenity. Instead of that reasonable expectation, we find ourselves at the conclusion of a war sacri-ficed to the indignation of our enemies, expelled our native country, and thrown on the wide world friendless and unsupported. It is needless to repeat the many promises of support and protection held out to the public by the King and those acting under his authority. These promises have been violated in every instance, and that national faith which we had been accustomed to look upon as sacred, basely bartered for an inglorious peace, even to this province which the loyalists from the other colonies have fled to for shelter, now denied us. The Spaniards are in a short time to take** possession of this province, and whilst we are together we had better draw up a decent petition to have protection, and throw ourselves on their mercy. If they deny us we will have few to condemn us, for what cruel and relenting necessity may compel us to adopt. Innumerable are the difficulties at present to encounter. Stripped of our property, drove from our homes, excluded from the company and care of our dearest connections, robbed of the blessing of a free and mild government, betrayed and deserted by our friends, what is it can repay us for our misery, dragging out a wretched life of obscurity and want? Heaven only that smooths the rugged paths of life can reconcile us to our misfortunes. Also, my hopes of ever receiving anything from Government for losses or services are vanished, as I cannot support any other opinion than whenever Great Britain sees it her interest to withdraw her force and protection from us, let us go where we will, we never can say we are safe from such difficulties as we have been induced to brave since the commencement of the late war, and for the same reason I shall in a few days get out in open boats to West Florida to settle myself at or near Fort Notches[148] on the Mississippi River."

On the 20th of March myself and seven other families set out, all in open boats. We kept company for 160 miles. I then left them and went forward to get to better hunting ground, and proceeded until I got to the Scibirsken,[149] where I waited for the rest of my company twelve days; but not seeing them come, I concluded they had passed me, and must have proceeded on their journey. I hoisted sail and stood on until I came to Key West, and seeing a large schooner I stood for her. She hove to, and when I came alongside she informed me that I was then on the edge of the Gulf of Mexico, and then I turned and stood for that key. I got to the key at three o'clock, and the wind blew a gale for fifteen days, and whilst on board the before-mentioned schooner, who belonged to the Spaniards. They had some Creek Indians on board, and then bound to Havana; the Spaniards I could not understand, but they understood the Creek language and my speaking to the Indians and informing of the Indians that I was going to Mississippi, he told me that my boat was too small, and it would be impossible for me to make the main land, as it was three days' sail before I could make land. The Spaniards understood all my discourse, and upon finding where I was bound, they spoke to me in Indian and told me that there were six or seven families of the English had left St. Augustine some time before, and that they were all killed except the negroes, and they thought we would stand a poor chance to escape them, as I should be obliged to keep the shore.

[148] Natchez.
[149] Key Biscayne.

In an hour after I made the key there came another Spanish schooner to anchor that I had passed the day before. They could not speak any English, but finding that the others could speak Creek, I also spoke to them in the same language, which they understood very well, and informed me as the other schooner had done. They were windbound for fifteen days, and treated me with every civility. I had one white lad of eighteen years of age, and by the different accounts we had of the Spaniards he got scared. I told him not to lose his life on my account. He then went on board of the schooner, and on the night the wind abated, the Spaniards came on shore and took the most of myself and wife's wearing apparel and bedding.

They informed me before their departure that they looked upon it that we could not proceed with our small open boats, the distance of the bay where we had to cross being about 36 leagues to a key called Sandy Key,[150] which is nine leagues from the main land, which in case of our not hitting that key the distance would be about 100 leagues before we should make land again. Upon which I turned and went back about twelve leagues to Key Bockes,[151] and steered due north till we made the key, being about eight hours out of sight of land. When we made the key, being 19th of said month, I got to said land the 20th. I saw a small schooner standing for the land about four leagues distance from us, and cast anchor where the aforementioned Spaniards informed us that the Indians were very bad in killing the English people that crossed the Bay of Tompay,[152] as the man that started with me being much alarmed at the behaviour of the Indians, set off back again with the Spaniards to the Havana. I then with my little family, consisting of my wife, self and two little negroes, I perceiving it might be dangerous for me to proceed, went on board the little schooner that lay at anchor about four leagues from me. I immediately took my boats and went on board of him, enquiring of one Baptist, who commanded her. I found he was an Italian; asked him where he was from, he informed me from New Providence. I then applied to him to get a passage with him. He told me he could not tell me at that time whether he could carry all my property or not, desired me to pay my boats off that night. The next morning he told me he could not give me a passage for less than 200 dollars. The next day he fell to 150 dollars. Then the wind blowing very fresh, I went on board my boat, and hoisted sail and went off for the land again. In the course of two or three hours he came round a point with a schooner to the land in order to mend some turtle nets which were much broken. He, during the time of his laying there, gave us liberty to come and sleep on board, and on the 23rd of the month I asked

---

[150] Sandy Key is a small island just south of Cape Sable.
[151] Boca Grande Key is an island west of Key West.
[152] Tampa.

him if he would not take less than 150 dollars to carry me to Providence, as I told him I could not afford to give him so much, as it was more than I was able to give him, as I was entirely robbed of what little I had. He said he would not take less. The next morning I set off in my boat and sent my girl along shore to catch some fowls I had on shore, where I was to come back again to the place as soon as I got the distance of about three miles round a point. When I got to the point I left my boat ashore, and went back in order to meet the girl where I expected to see her. I got about half the distance, but did not meet her, and coming there and not finding her I went some little distance back to where the schooner lay. As I expected, they were going to use me in the same manner the Spaniards had done before, when I saw them take my negro girl and carry her on board with them. I then sat down for the space of a half hour, and considering within myself what I had best do, and seeing the said Baptist, commander of the said schooner, and his man Thomas coming ashore again, after carrying my negro girl off into the woods and hid her. I then saw them coming out of the woods. Thinking within myself that they intended to kill me, with which I looked and examined my gun and powder; finding I had only one charge with me or nigher than my boats, and considering the present distressed situation I was in, obliged me to consider what was my best measure to pursue, and I immediately advanced towards them, they parting, one turned back to where the girl was, the other coming on a small distance, went from the beach and turned off into the woods. I immediately ran and called to him and asked him concerning what he had done with the girl, with which he denied having seen her. I then told him he need not deny it, for I had seen him with her, and offered him four dollars if he would inform me where she was, so that I could get her. He immediately said that Mr. Baptist had the command of the schooner, and that I had better go back and speak to him myself. I also went back to where their boat lay, and continued there for the space of fifteen minutes, then I turned and walked back from the place I started from. During the course of my walking I looked behind and saw the said Baptist about 150 yards in my rear, his gun lying across his left arm. I turned around and advanced to him, and when near him I observed his gun cocked. I asked him at first what he had his gun cocked for; his answer was in order to fire at anything that came. With that I told him that he had better uncock his gun as I did not see anything to fire at there. I told him several times; he replied he always carried his gun cocked, and kept her cocked for the space of fifteen minutes. I asked if he had not seen my girl come that way. He told me no. I then told him that he need not deny it, for I had seen her on board his boat, he being in the boat at the same time, carrying her off to the schooner, not mentioning to him that I saw him bring her back. I then told him I could carry him back and show him the girl's tracks where he had carried her along and took her on board. I then offered him four dollars to give her up, as I told him my present situations would not admit of my giving him as much money as he asked to carry me to Providence. He told me I talked like a boy, as no person would carry me to Providence under five hundred dollars, and he only asked one hundred and fifty, and also alluded to my going off and not speaking to him any more, and that if he had my girl he would keep her as he had lost a boy that cost him eight hundred dollars, and that he must make something before he returned to Providence. I asked him if he would carry me for either the boy or girl, allowing me fifty dollars. He told me no. I told him that it was but little less than the half I was worth; he told me he would carry me for one of them, or fifty dollars. In my distressed situation, and my wife being pregnant, I thought I had best endeavour to get a passage with him. I told him that I would sooner than to lose my negro girl give him one hundred and fifty dollars than either the girl or the boy, as I was convinced I should have justice done me on my arrival at New Providence, as I should see some persons who were acquainted with me in Providence; he told me he would. I then told him I wanted him to drop his schooner down to where my boats were in order to get my property out of the boats. He told me he could not as he was going round the Key to turtle. I then going back, I met with the other man and wanted to hire him. He told me he could not unless I had got liberty from Baptist. With that I went myself, and came to my boats and told my wife the situation of matters, and we immediately started with only my boy's assistance and rowed back against the wind blowing fresh for seven miles; then coming very near the schooner I threw out my anchor and lay there all night, and the next morning I called to them several times and asked them if they had seen my girl. After some time they answered me, Ay, Ay! and told us to come alongside. I told them I wanted my girl to come and assist me in taking out my property. They answered me they would assist me in taking them out. With that I weighed anchor and went alongside of the schooner and told my wife to go on board. When on board she went and called the girl several times. My wife then went down into the hold with a stick, and she said that she found the girl hid among the sails, being stripped of all her clothes she had on the day when she left me. I had my property put on board, and soon after I set off to the shore and anchored my large boat some little distance from the shore, where I lay till some time in June, round the point where I came from, as the wind was blowing fresh. On the 15th of June he got his turtle and water on board where he had his turtle in a crawl in the Bay of Fundy, where he had supplied himself with wood and water, and all his turtle on board, where he then drew a note of hand for me to sign for two hundred pieces of eight for my passage. I immediately answered him I would sooner suffer death than to sign any instrument of writing. He then wished himself damned before I should go with him, and ordered me to haul up my boat and put what I could in her and go on shore with my family. My boat being so small would not carry one-fourth part of my property off. As there lay a large boat alongside that they had brought off their turtle wood and water on board in, I asked them for the loan of her. They told me they could not as they were going to get under way. With that I brought my boat alongside, and they in the meantime took their two boats and went on shore. My wife being in a bad situation, fell a crying and begged of me to do anything to get away for fear we might meet with others who might distress us of everything. As I found that I should lose the greatest part in case I went on shore, as I had left my large boat at Cape Sable[153] on the mainland, and my little boat not being large enough to contain over the one-fourth of my property, for which I told him to draw a note for one hundred and fifty dollars, for which I signed, the note being dated 15th July, and was to be paid after my arrival in Providence, to have thirty-five days after my landing there before payment was to be made.

On the 30th of June, as we were laying at New Madamcumba[154] after our having several words, he told me that he understood by my negroes that I intended to have him hung after my arrival at New Providence if he had turned my wife on shore, and in case she had died that I should do my endeavours to hang him in Providence, and told me if it had not been for killing my wife he would be damned if he did not drown me overboard long ago, only on account of my wife. On the 12th July a Capt. Bunch, Capt. Clutsam, and Capt. Wm. Smith, of New Providence, appeared, and Capt. Bunch came on board the small schooner commanded by the said Baptist. The said Mr. Bunch asked me my reasons for staying so long on board that small schooner, and why I gave the said Baptist my note of hand for one hundred and fifty dollars, of which Mr. Bunch informed me that it was contrary to the laws of the Government of New Providence to make any agreement with any person or persons found in distress, but to render every assistance. With this I found Mr. Bunch wished to render me a service in my distressed situation, and I opened to him all former proceedings respecting the ill treatment and behaviour of the said Baptist. On the same account every gentleman of them offered me any assistance I wanted, and

---

[153] Cape Sable is a peninsula on the southwest coast of Florida, now in the Everglades National Park.

[154] New Matecumbe referred to one of the Florida Keys. There are two keys by this name today—Upper and Lower Matecumbe.

Mr. Bunch told me that in case I did not get a passage with Capt. Clutsam, which he did not doubt but what I should, he would give me a passage himself. However, I procured a passage from Capt. Clutsam for fifty dollars, during which passage I was in every respect used and treated like a gentleman by the said Capt. Clutsam, and on my arrival at New Providence the said Capt. Clutsam behaved with so much honour that, instead of taking fifty dollars of me, he deducted twenty, and only charged me thirty, and upon finding who I was would not take but twenty dollars, and he at the same time refused taking any more of me. During the course of my being on board of Capt. Clutsam he found me in every necessary, and made no charge for any provisions or anything I received from him. His humanity was so great, that if ever in my power to render any service to him or any of those gentlemen, nothing shall ever be wanting on my part to do them service.

I continued in Nassau for twenty days, and then took my passage with Capt. Jacob Bell to New Brunswick, where we cast anchor 23rd of Sept., 1784, and continued until the 25th of October, and then set out for Halifax to his Excellency Governor Parr,[155] to know how I should get land, but as I got to Halifax his Excellency Governor Carlton arrived, and I could do nothing, so I returned on the 7th November, and in August I received the following letter from Col. John Hamilton in answer to mine in regard to my claims:

Dear Sir—I received yours of the 9th February, 1785, a few days ago and notice the contents. I am sorry to inform you that your claims are not yet given in, but I expect the office for receiving claims will be opened again by act of Parliament this session, when you may depend proper care shall be taken of yours. I am sorry to hear of your losses. I hope you are now agreeably settled, and making something for your family. I think if you can leave your business in proper hands, a trip to this country would be of service to you, though I don't think you would get half-pay. Government would settle an annuity on you for life; which cannot be done without your coming here.

If you come you may depend on all my interest in your favour, and I

[155] JOHN PARR (1725-1791), a native of Ireland, entered the British army in 1744 and was promoted to lieutenant colonel in 1771. In 1782 he was appointed governor of the province of Nova Scotia. The influx of Loyalist immigrants led to the formation of New Brunswick from Nova Scotia in 1784, and Parr became lieutenant governor of the present province of Nova Scotia. St. John, N.B., was originally named Parrtown. W. Stewart Wallace, *The MacMillan Dictionary of Canadian Biography* (3rd ed.; Toronto: MacMillan, 1963), pp. 581–82.

cannot help thinking it worth your while to come home.

I am, dear sir, your humble servant,

John Hamilton.

London, May 10th, 1785.

In a short time after I heard that there was another act of Parliament passed to receive claims for losses and services, also that the Commissioners had arrived at Halifax, and on the 20th March, I set out for Halifax, and presented a copy of my claim from East Florida, with the Memorial as follows:

"To the Honourable Commissioners, appointed by act of Parliament, further to enquire into the losses and services of the American Loyalists.

The Memorial of David Fanning, late Colonel of the North Carolina Militia, humbly sheweth: That your Memorialist is a loyalist from North Carolina, who uniformly and religiously adhered to his duty and loyalty to the best of Sovereigns, for which he suffered persecution, and many other inconveniences—that your Memorialist, by a warrant from Major Craig, of the 82nd Regiment, then commanding at Wilmington, was placed at the head of the militia of that province; that your Memorialist during the late war did command from one to nine hundred and fifty men, with whom he was engaged in six and thirty skirmishes in North Carolina, and four in South Carolina; all of which were of his own planning and in which he had the honour to command; that your Memorialist killed many of the rebels and took many of them prisoners; among the latter of whom were Governor Burke, his council, and many officers of distinction in the rebel army; that your Memorialist, during that time, was twice wounded, and fourteen times taken prisoner; that, on the conclusion of the late peace, your Memorialist settled two hundred and fifty souls in East Florida; and himself having taken refuge in several parts of his Majesty's remaining possessions in America, finally settled in the Province of New Brunswick, where he is in great distress, with his family. That your Memorialist, in consequence of his said loyalty to his Sovereign, the many services rendered him, and attachment to the British Government, had his property, real and personal, seized, confiscated, and sold by rebel authority. Your Memorialist therefore prays that his case may be taken into consideration, in order that he may be enabled under your report to receive such aid or relief as his case may be found to deserve."

David Fanning.

St. John, March 1st, 1786.

I also took the following oath before Peter Hunter, Secretary to the Commissioners, in favour of my claim at Halifax:

Town of Halifax,   S.S.
    Nova Scotia.

David Fanning, late of North Carolina, Colonel of Militia, but now of Kings County, in the Province of New Brunswick, maketh oath and saith that he resided in East Florida and the Bahama Islands from the 15th day of July, 1783, to the 25th of March, 1784, and this deponent further saith that he was utterly incapable of preferring or delivering to the Commissioners appointed by Act of Parliament passed in the twenty-third year of his present Majesty entitled an Act for appointing Commissioners to enquire into the losses and services of all such persons who have suffered in their rights, properties and possessions, during the late unhappy dissensions in America in consequence of their loyalty to his Majesty and attachment to the British Government, or at this office any Memorial Claim or request for aid or relief on account of this deponent's losses during the late unhappy dissensions in America, within the limited time by the said Act for the receiving of such claims by the reason that this deponent during all such time, viz., Between the 15th July, 1783, and the 25th March, 1784, lived or resided in East Florida and the Bahama Islands; that this deponent did, however, send a claim to Col. John Hamilton, of the North Carolina Volunteers in England, of his losses, but that by a letter that this deponent received from said Hamilton, bearing date 10th May, 1785, he is informed that his claims were not then given to the Commissioners in England, and that this deponent believes his said claim must have arrived in London after the time appointed by the late Act of Parliament for receiving such claims had expired, or that the Colonel, Hutchins, to whom I had entrusted the delivery of the said claim had neglected the trust reposed in him in giving in my claim.

Sworn this _____ day of March, 1786, before me—
                                David Fanning.

When I presented my Memorial and estimate of claim to Peter Hunter, Secretary to the Commissioners, he gave me no manner of satisfaction, and on my asking him if I could come under an examination, he told me to be gone, he did not think the Commissioners would receive my claim. When I found I could get no hearing at Halifax at that time, I returned home with a full resolution never to trouble myself any more. At the time of being in Halifax I met my old friend, Capt. John Legett, of the Royal North Carolina Regiment, who said he would speak to the Commissioners in my favour. He also gave me a copy of the following letter from Lieut.-Col. Arch. McKay:

London, Nov. 15th. 1785.

Dear Captain,—

Ever mindful of your good-will and the kindness you showed unto me since I had the pleasure of being acquainted with you, induces me to write you a few lines at present informing you of my success since I came to England, knowing you would be glad to hear of the provision made for me. When I came to England, I got a hearing by the Commissioners of American Claims, and they granted me thirty pounds yearly for temporary subsistence. I then laid in a memorial to Sir George Young for Captain's half-pay; but I must confess I thought my chances for that bad enough, as I was not acquainted with any of the Generals who commanded in America; but since it was only amusement to try, I got a certificate from Col. Craig, and another from Col. Hamilton and laid them in with the memorial. It was, with a good many others, a long time from office to office; at length they have allowed me seventy pounds sterling, yearly, for life, for my services in America, exclusive of the other thirty pounds. Upon the whole I do not repent coming to London, as things have turned out.

I wrote to Capt. McNeill this morning, not thinking I should have time to write to you before the ship sailed, and I had not time to write to him so fully as I could wish, but I will mind better next time.

I intend to spend next summer in Scotland, if everything turns out here to my expectations, and I would be glad to get a long letter from you concerning your new settlements. You will please to write to me, under cover to Messrs. John and Hector McKay, No. 5, Crown Court, Westminster; and if I am in Britain I shall be sure to get any letter that may come for me. After my jaunt to Scotland I hope to do myself the honour to call and see you on my way to New Providence, where Alexander and Malcom McKay are gone. I am, sir, with due respect,

Your sincere friend and humble servant,

Archibald McKay."

To Capt. John Legett.

I returned home and continued until the 27th June, 1787. When I was entering the suburbs of the city of St. John, I accidentally met Ensign Henry Niss, with a letter from the Commissioners, desiring me to attend immediately for an examination. I still retained my opinion, but on informing Col. Joseph Robinson, he prevailed with me, after a long persuasion, to call and see the Commissioners, which I did, in company with Col. Robinson, where I was treated with every civility and all attention paid to me. After my examination they gave me the following certificate:

"Office of American Claims,
St. John, 2nd February, 1787.

We do hereby certify that David Fanning has undergone an examination on oath before us, as an American sufferer from North Carolina. We are satisfied by his own account, and by the evidence he has produced, that his exertions in support of the British Government, as Colonel of the Chatham and Randolph County Militia, during the late troubles in America, have been very great and exemplary; that he has been severely wounded in several engagements and has in other respects been a great sufferer; though from particular reasons, it will not be in our power to make him any considerable allowance under our report. We therefore recommend him as a proper person to be put on the half-pay list as Captain and to have an annual allowance from Government equal to that half-pay.

Thomas Dundas.
J. Pemberton."

I then empowered George Randall, Esq., Whitehall, London, to act for me. I sent the original certificates and memorial in company with the letter.

To the Right Honorable Sir George Younge, Baronet, Secretary at War, etc. etc.:

The Memorial of David Fanning, late Colonel of the Chatham and Randolph County Militia, in North Carolina, humbly sheweth:

That in the year 1781, under an appointment from Major Henry Craig, then commanding the British troops in North Carolina, your Memorialist embodied near one thousand men of the loyal inhabitants of that Province, and with them performed singular service to the British Government; that he has been twice severely wounded in the course of the war; he has been fourteen times taken prisoner, and has been tried for his life by the rebels and has ever exerted his utmost endeavours in support of the cause of Great Britain; he is disabled by wounds he has received and has no means of support. For the truth of these allegations he begs to refer to his appointment of Colonel, to the certificates of several officers under whom he served, and to the certificates of the Commissioners of American Claims, forwarded herewith.

Your Memorialist most humbly prays that he may be put on the Provincial half-pay list as Captain, fully confident that his past services and present necessitous situation will be thought deserving of that appointment, and your Memorialist, as in duty bound, shall ever pray,

David Fanning.

City of St. John, 2nd February, 1787.

Pursuant to the advice of Lieut.-Col. Joseph Robinson, I have transmitted a power of attorney to you in order to receive half-pay, with a certificate from the Commissioners. Mr. I. Pemberton and Colonel Dundas, Esq.; General Alexander Leslie, Col. Nisbet Balfour, Lieut.-Col. J. Henry Craig, of the 16th Regiment, and Lieut-Col. John Hamilton, of the North Carolina Regiment, are witnesses of my services. If you will be so good as to accept the power and grant me your assistance in obtaining the same, you will highly oblige,

Sir, your most obedient humble servant,

David Fanning.

New Brunswick,

City of St. John, February 7th, 1787.

George Randall, Esq., Westminster, Whitehall, London.

Received July 20th, 1787, the following from my agent:

Whitehall, 15th May, 1787.

Sir—On the 3rd inst., in a letter to Lieut.-Col. Robinson, I desired he would inform you of my having received your Memorial, Certificate, etc., claiming the half-pay of a Captain or a military pension equal to the rank. Since then I have received your letter with duplicates of the above papers, and your bill of £260 1s. has been presented as you desired, and as I was also much disposed to do. I gave the holder a favourable answer and the true one, that you had reason to expect that I should have effects in hand sufficient to pay the bill when it became due, but that a delay in settling your business and which you could not foresee, would for a time prevent my accepting your bill.

I must now inform you that I took the earliest opportunity of presenting your memorial and the certificate of the Commissioners, being highly honourable to you and recommending you for an allowance, or the half-pay of Captain. I think there is no reason to doubt you will have a sum equal to that rank allowed you by Government. You had omitted to request that the grant might take place from the 24th of October, 1783, but I added a paragraph to the memorial for that purpose, but whether you will be allowed from that period is doubtful. I am sorry at the same time to acquaint you that it may be some months before the determination of Government is known but you may be sure that I shall pay a particular attention to your business and give you the earliest notice of the event. The certificate you sent, though very regular as to the periods, I think would not entitle me to receive the money from the pay office on your account, as I am inclined to believe your allowance will be a military allowance, and not half-pay, and for that reason I send you a printed certificate, which you can keep as a precedent, and desire you will transmit to me a sett, copied from it, for the same periods as them you have already transmitted, taking particular care that there be no blot, alteration or erasure in the dates. I will be much obliged to you if you will acquaint Chillas that the answer of Government to his memorial is that he cannot be placed on the half-pay establishment, the commission he held being only in the militia of the town of New York.

The packet you sent with the certificate amounted to 12 shillings postage and your single letter to one shilling.

I am, sir, your most obedient humble servant,

George Randall.

To David Fanning.

Whitehall, 1st August, 1787.

Sir,—On the 15th May, I acknowledged the receipt of your letter and duplicate containing memorials, certificates and other papers relating to your claim of half-pay, or a military pension, and acquainted you that having presented those papers, I thought you had a very fair prospect of success. I am still of that opinion, but am sorry to acquaint you that the consideration of half-pay claims is again deferred and that it may be some months longer before I can acquaint you with the results. I conclude, therefore, that the bill you drew on me for £260 1s. must be returned.

I have received from the Treasury the sum granted to you by Government on account of your losses, for which I gave a receipt in the annexed form and am ready to accept your bill for £22 14s., as after deducting agency and postage, etc., and abstract herewith sent.

Copy of a receipt:

The 24th day of July, 1787, received of Mr. Thomas Coffin by order of the Lords of the Treasury and according to a distribution under the direction of the Commissioners of American Claims, appointed by an Act of the 23rd of his present Majesty, the sum of £24, as a payment for present relief and on account of the losses during the late dissensions in America.

Signed for David Fanning,

£24 0s.   G. Randall, Attorney.

After this I received the letter from my Agent and found I had lost property to the amount of £1,625 10s. according to an appraisement of three men acquainted with the property. But, as it was not like a coat taken out of my hand, or gold taken out of my pocket, I could not get anything for my losses, although I did not give in anything like the amount of my losses. I lost twenty-four horses, and only reported fifteen, one of which cost more than all I ever got from Government, and six head of cattle, £289 for property sold at the commencement of the war, and the land which I was heir to, and for which I refused, many times, £3,000 Virginia currency. But because I turned out in the service of my King and country in the 20th year of my age, and my exertions were very exemplary in support of the British Government, I have lost my all, for and on account of my attachment to the British Government—only £60, which would not pay the expenses I have been at to obtain it.

I can prove what I have here wrote to be facts, and the world will be able to judge after reading this narrative, and observe this Act of Oblivion passed in North Carolina, in the year 1783, which is herewith set forth—which is enlarged and improved in the *London Magazine*, which will be found on page 607, Vol. 1, from July 1 to Dec. 1, 1783.

An Act of Pardon and Oblivion, by the State of North Carolina.

Whereas, it is the policy of all wise States, on the termination of all Civil Wars, to grant an Act of Pardon and Oblivion for past offences, and as divers of the citizens of this State and others, the inhabitants thereof in the course of the late unhappy war, have become liable to great pains and penalties for offences committed against the peace and government of this State, and the General Assembly, out of an earnest desire to observe the articles of peace on all occasions, disposed to forgive offences rather than punish where the necessity for an exemplary punishment has ceased. Be it therefore enacted by the General Assembly of the State of North Carolina, and it is hereby enacted by the authority of the same, that all and all manner of treasons, misprisions of treason, felony or misdemeanour, committed or done since the 4th day of July, 1776, by any persons whatsoever, be pardoned, released and put in total oblivion.

Provided always that this Act or anything therein contained, shall not extend to pardon or discharge, or give any benefit whatsoever to persons who have taken commission or have been denominated officers, and acted as such to the King of Great Britain, or to such as are named in any of the laws commonly called confiscation laws, or to such as have attached themselves to the British and continued without the limits of the State and not returned within twelve months previous to the passing of this Act.

Provided further, that nothing herein contained shall extend to pardon Peter Mallet, David Fanning and Samuel Andrews, or any person or persons guilty of deliberate and wilful murder, robbery, rape or housebreaking, or any of them, anything herein contained to the contrary notwithstanding. Provided, nevertheless, that nothing in this Act shall be construed to bar any citizen of this State from their civil action for the recovery of debts or damage. Provided, also, that nothing herein contained shall entitle any person by this law to be relieved to elect or be elected to any office or trust in this State, or to hold any office civil or military.

And whereas by an Act passed at Wake Court House, all officers, civil and military, who have taken parole were suspended from the execution of their respective offices, and required to appear at the next General Assembly, to shew cause, if any they could, why they should not be removed from the said office; and, whereas, several of the officers aforesaid have neglected to appear agreeably to the requisition of the Act of Assembly. Be it enacted by the General Assembly of the State of North Carolina, and it is hereby enacted, by the authority of the same, that all such officers, both civil and military, are hereby declared to stand suspended from the execution of their several offices until they shall appear at some future Assembly and be restored to the execution of their respective offices or removed agreeable to their merits or demerits. Provided that nothin herein contained shall be construed to exclude a Justice of the Peace from executing the duties of his office, who shall make it appear to the satisfaction of the Court of his County by oath or otherwise; that he was taken prisoner without his consent and privily, and that after his capture he had not voluntarily stayed with the enemy, nor taken an active part in any manner by furnishing them willingly with provisions, bearing arms, or accepting any appointment in their civil regulations.

Read three times and ratified in General Assembly, the 17th May, 1783.

Ric. Caswell, S. Senate.
E. Starkey, S. Commons.

Many people are fools enough to think, because our three names are particularly put in this Act, that we are all guilty of the crimes set forth, but I defy the world to charge me with rape, or anything more than I have set forth in this Journal.

All his Majesty's subjects or others that wish to know the truth of anything further than I have set forth, let them make enquiry of those gentlemen whose names I have struck in; examine the letters of the rebels, and the recommendations of the officers who have been acquainted with me in person and with my services in the time of the late war.

Although I have been prohibited from receiving any benefit from the laws of the State, all that I desire is to have the liberty of commanding 30,000 men in favour of the British Government. I flatter myself that there would be no doubt of my putting many of them to swing by the neck for their honesty, as John White did, after stealing 150 horses in North Carolina.

Appendix

THE FOLLOWING documents from the Manuscripts Division of the Library of Congress are a letter from General John Butler to Governor Thomas Burke of March 6, 1782, which accompanied David Fanning's letter to the governor of February 26, 1782. The truce conditions were included in Fanning's letter and were copied into Fanning's journal, appearing in the Jonas Howe transcription (see pp. 68–70). The letter of February 26 is in Fanning's handwriting, and the portion of the letter containing the truce conditions is the only part of the journal that survives in its original state. It is obvious when comparing the Howe transcription with the original letter that Fanning refined his journal as he wrote it. There is evidence of at least two versions of the journal—the first being the one dated by Fanning in 1790 and the second being the version Howe described as dictated to and copied by Ferebee Fanning. Copies of the following letters from the Executive Letter Book were published in Clark, *State Records*, XVI, 205–8, 217. The present transcriptions are based on the originals in the Library of Congress.

Mount Pleasant   6th March 1782
Dear Sir
    Inclosed is four letters, one from Col. Fanning, one from Capt Golson, one from Major Griffith, and one from Col. Oneal—I take Fannings to be a very ridiculous piece tho I doubt not that he is in Earnest and the tenour of it, Golsons & Major Griffiths, seems to prove the necessity of posting the State Troops at Different Stations on Deep River, as you mentioned at Halifax the [intelligence] convey^d in Oneals   I begin to doubt the truth of, I hope you will Excuse me for Troubling your Excellency with these letters, for tho they Contain nothing of real consequence yet I thought it my duty to let you see them, I have the honour to be your Excellencies most obedient Servant——
                         John Butler

Governor Burke
Recd Mch 25th 1782
    ansd Sameday

John Butler to Thomas Burke, March 6, 1782.
United States Revolution, Miscellany, 1774–1783, Manuscripts Division, Library of Congress, Washington, D.C.

To his Excelency Cpt General Commander In Cheaf or the Nex Offacer In Command

Sir

I Undstand that you have hung three of My Men one Cpt and two Privates and Likewise have a Cpt and Six Men Under the Sentance of Death[.] Sir If the Requestion of My Artacles Do Not Arive to Satisfaction and the affusion of Blood Stopt and the Lives of those Men Saved that I will Retaliate Blood for Blood and ten fold for one and their Shall Never A Offacer or Private of the Rebel Party Escape that falls Into My hands hereafter But what shall Suffer the Pains and Punnishments of Instant Death[.] I have got your Proclamations whareas It Specifies this that all offacers Leading Men persons of this Class Gilty of Murder Roberry and houseBurning to Be Precluded from any Benefits of your Proclamation for their Never was a man thats Been In Arms on Either Side But what Is gilty of Some of the Above Mentioned Crimes Espacially on the Reble Side and them thats Guilty Is to Suffer Instant Death If taken[.] If My Request Agreable to My Artales ant granted and Arive By the Eighth Day of March Next that I Shall fall Upon the Saverest and Most unhumanest Tirms Emaginable to Answer the Ends for Satisfaction for those that are So Executed[.] If the Request Is Granted Amediately Send a Feald Offacer to Deep River to Mr winsor Pearce and there he May Remain [illegible] or to Colo Phillap Alstons under a flag till we Can Settle the Matter[.] So No More But I am In Behalf of his Majestys Troop your Most humble Servent

David Fanning   Colo
Commander of the Loyal Malitia of Randolph & Chatham
Fabuery th 26 1782

On Friday the Seventh of January Last I wrote to Lawer williams the tirms that I was willing to Surrender Under & he wrote to Me that general Butler Could not Comply With my tirms till he had the Approbation of the Governor. on Wensday the Eleventh Instant the Flag was to Meet me At a Sertain house With the Letter And As the flag Was Comming It was waylaid By Charls Goldson and A Party of Men for which It apeared to Me that they Send more Like taking My Life By treachery than Comeing Upon Peacable tirms But as the Gentleman that Bare the flag Balam Tomson Acting So Onerable to his trust the Minnet he Arived at the Place he Let me know Of It and Declared himself Innosent which Gave Me Ground to think he would Act with honner Still

on the fifteenth of the Instant Mr williams Mr Clark and Mr Burns was the Gentlemen that was Cind anuf to weight Upon Me with a Blank Perole and Letter that My Request was Granted By the Govener[.] In the Mean time the Gentlemen waighting on me at the Place Appointed[,] there Came Round A Company from the haw fealds Commanded By Cpt Scobe which Plainly and Evedently Apeared to Me that their was Nothing but treachery meant[.] on Sundy the 10 of fabuary I fell In the Rear of Cpt Coldson & Capt hinds & following their trail Came on them at Dusk & after Some fireing that Night we Rode of & Came on them Next morning and we Came Upon tirms of Peace till I Could write to their Superiors for which I have Counceled with Some of My Offacers & We Goined with hand & hart to Comply with the tirms Underneath Riten

we the Subscribers Do Acknolege ourselves Subjects to the British Government as you are well asured of our fedility and Loyalty to his Majesty and It has Been Dayley the Case that we have Been Destroying one anothers Persons and Property to Uphold our Opinions and we are hereby willing to Come to a Session of Arms for three Months and the Condition Under writen

our Request is from Cumberland twenty Miles North and thirty Miles East and west to Be totle Clear of Any of your Light horse

and further that Every Man that has Been In Actual Arms In A Pirmanent Order. In Order to Establish A Royal Goverment Exceptting those that have Deserted from a regular Trupe who have Vollentaraly Inlisted themselves them we Do Obligate to Deliver Up & Each and Every Man that are at Liberty Shall have a wright to withdraw themselves In the Sd District

and that any Person Living In Sd District that have Not Been In Actual Arms In a Permanent manner to Establish the Royal Goverment that we Should at Any Request By Writing to Me or Major Reins have them Apprehended and Sent to any of the Amarican offacers At or Near the Line

that If any of our Men Should Go out of the Line or District to Plunder or Destress or Murder Any of the Amarican's Party that we will By Infermation Made to Me or Major Reins or any of the Cpts that I Shall Return their Names[.] If they Request Is Granted that they Shall Emediately Be Aprehended And Sent to you or the Nearest Offacer to Be tried By your own Law

and If any of your Party Shall Be Cetcht Plundering Stealing or Murdering or Going Private Paths With Arms Signifing as If they Ware for Mischeaf to Be Left to Our Pleasure to Deal with as We se Cause Agreable to Our Law[.] All Public Rodes to Be free to Be traviled By any Army or Company Ceping [keeping] the Pubic Rode or Waggons

that Every Person that has Been In Actual Arms In a Perminent manner In order to Establish the Royal Goverment Shall not Be Interrupted Of their Arms or Provision[.] And Any Person that has Not Been In Arms As Above Riten If you Should want Provision or any Other Article from them to send to Either of Us and we will send a suffitiant Gard to se them Safe In and out[,] the quakers Excepted[,] and that we Will Not In the Mean Time Distress nor Disturb any Person abiding By your Law In the Sd District In their Person or Property

all Back Plunder Shall Be Void as It Is Inposable to Replace and Restore All the Plunder on any Side

our Request Is to have a free trade to Any Party with wagans or hors Back without arms with a Pass from any apointed offacer for Salt or Iron or any other necessary

and we Except the two Coxes Mils to Be free from all armies Belonging to America

any Man that has Been Returned A Continental without takeing the Bounty that has Been In Actual Arms as Above Mentioned Shall Return In the S^d District

If the Request Is Granted Above Reten I Should Request the Liberty to Send to Charlstown to Let them know what we are about and any Request you Should Ask In Reason I will Petition for and Perhaps A Peace might Be made for a twelve Month or More If you Desire It

If the Request Canot Be Granted Be Pleased to Let Me Know as quick as Possable and If You Dont Like to Comply with our tirms Send Me an Answer Back amediately that we May know what to Depend Upon So No More At Present But we Remain Friends In Behalf of his Majistys Troops[.] Sir we Remain your faithfull humble Sarvents

The Signers names on the other Side
David Fanning Col
John Reins Major
William Reins Capt
John Cagle Capt
William Price Capt
Jacob Manes Insign

[address]
To his Excellency governor Commander In Cheaf of the State
Thomas Buirk or the Next Commander at hand

David Fanning to Thomas Burke, February 26, 1782.
United States Revolution, Miscellany, 1774–1783, Manuscripts Division, Library of Congress, Washington, D.C.

Bibliography

PRIMARY SOURCES

Manuscripts

Audit Office Papers, 1765–90, American Loyalist Claims. Public Record Office, London. Transcripts of North Carolina Claims in Division of Archives and History, Raleigh. Transcripts of South Carolina Claims in New York Public Library. Microfilm copy in South Carolina Department of Archives and History, Columbia, S. C.

Thomas J. Clay Papers, 1737–1927, Vol. I. Manuscripts Division, Library of Congress, Washington, D.C.

Colonial Land Plats, South Carolina Department of Archives and History, Columbia, S. C.

Confiscated Estates: Lists of Loyalists, 1783. South Carolina Department of Archives and History, Columbia, S. C.

Cornwallis Papers. Public Record Office, London. Microfilm in Manuscripts Division, Library of Congress, Washington, D.C.

Delamar Transcripts: Legislative Papers Relating to Revolution Service. Division of Archives and History, Raleigh, N. C.

David Fanning Letter. Public Archives of Nova Scotia, Halifax, N. S.

Fanning Family Papers. Archives of the New Brunswick Museum, St. John, N. B.

Munson Jarvis Papers. Archives of the New Brunswick Museum, St. John, N. B.

"A Journal of Col^n David Fannings transactions During the late War in America, from the year 1775—Commencing 1^{ts} of May until the peace." Jonas Howe transcript. Archives of the New Brunswick Museum, St. John, N. B.

Land Petitions, Warrants, Grants, Escheats, and Unused Petitions, 1783–1810. Public Archives of Nova Scotia, Halifax, N. S.

Archibald DeBow Murphey Papers. Southern Historical Collection, University of North Carolina Library, Chapel Hill, N. C.

Revolutionary Records, Audited Accounts. South Carolina Department of Archives and History, Columbia, S. C.

Revolutionary War Pension and Bounty Land Warrant Application Files. National Archives Microfilm Publications. Microfilm in South Carolina Department of Archives and History, Columbia, S. C.

Alfred W. Savary Letters. North Carolina Collection, University of North Carolina Library, Chapel Hill, N. C.

David Lowry Swain Papers, 1801–68. Southern Historical Collection, University of North Carolina Library, Chapel Hill, N. C.

United States Revolution, Miscellany, 1774–83. Manuscripts Division, Library of Congress, Washinton, D.C.

Local Records

Chatham County Court Minutes, 1774–84. Division of Archives and History, Raleigh, N. C.

Chatham County Deeds. Register of Deeds, Pittsboro, N. C.

Chatham County Wills. Clerk of Superior Court, Pittsboro, N. C.

Cumberland County Court Minutes, 1777–81. Division of Archives and History, Raleigh, N. C.

Digby County Wills. Office of the Register of Probate, Digby, N. S.

Guilford County Deeds. Register of Deeds, Greensboro, N. C.

Guilford County Wills. Clerk of Superior Court, Greensboro, N. C.

Johnston County Court Minutes, 1764. Division of Archives and History, Raleigh, N. C.

Orange County Court Minutes, 1781–82. Division of Archives and History, Raleigh, N. C.

Orange County Deeds. Register of Deeds, Hillsborough, N. C.

Orange County Wills, Clerk of Superior Court, Hillsborough, N. C.

Queens County Deeds, Queens County Registry Office. Microfilm in Public Archives of New Brunswick, Fredericton, N. B.

Randolph County Court Minutes, 1779–82. Division of Archives and History, Raleigh, N. C.

Rowan County Deeds. Microfilm in Division of Archives and History, Raleigh, N. C.

Published Documents, Narratives, and Newspapers

Clark, Walter M. (ed.). *The State Records of North Carolina*. 16 vols. Winston and Goldsboro, N. C.: State of North Carolina, 1895–1906.

Fraser, Alexander (comp.). Ontario Bureau of Archives, *Second Report*. Toronto: L. K. Cameron, 1905.

Gibbes, R. W. (ed.). *Documentary History of the American Revolution: Consisting of Letters and Papers Relating to the Contest for Liberty, Chiefly in South Carolina, from originals in the Possession of the Editor, and other Sources, 1764–1776*. New York: D. Appleton & Company, 1855.

Heads of Families at the First Census of the United States in the Year 1790: North Carolina. Baltimore, Md.: Genealogical Publishing Co. [reprint edition], 1966.

Hemphill, Wiliam Edwin, and Wylma Anne Wates (eds.). *The State Records of South Carolina: Extracts from the Journals of the Provincial Congresses, 1775–1776*. Columbia, S. C.: South Carolina Archives, 1960.

Hemphill, William Edwin, Wylma Anne Wates, and R. Nicholas Olsberg (eds.). *The State Records of South Carolina: Journals of the General Assembly and the House of Representatives, 1776–1780*. Columbia, S. C.: University of South Carolina Press, 1970.

Hoyt, William H. (ed.). *The Papers of Archibald D. Murphey*. 2 vols. Raleigh, N. C.: North Carolina Historical Commission, 1914.

Linn, Jo White, and B. R. McBride (comps.). "Delamar Revolutionary Pension Abstracts," *North Carolina Genealogical Society Journal*, II (April, 1976), 108.

McEachern, Leora H., and Isabel M. Williams (eds.). *Wilmington-New Hanover Safety Committee Minutes, 1774–1776*. Wilmington, N. C.: Wilmington-New

Hanover American Revolution Bi-centennial Association, 1974.

Reese, George H. (comp.). *The Cornwallis Papers: Abstracts of Americana.* Charlottes-ville, Va.: University of Virginia Press, 1970.

"Rules and Regulations For the well-governing the Loyal Militia of the Province of *North-Carolina.*" Wilmington, September 25, 1781. North Carolina Collecttion, University of North Carolina Library, Chapel Hill, N. C.

Salley, A. S., Jr. (ed.). *Stub Entries to Indents Issued in Payment of Claims Against South Carolina Growing out of the Revolution.* Columbia, S. C.: Historical Commission of South Carolina, 1925.

Saunders, William L. (ed.). *The Colonial Records of North Carolina.* 10 vols. Raleigh, N. C.: State of North Carolina, 1886–90.

Savary, Alfred W. (ed.). *Col. David Fanning's Narrative of his Exploits and Adventures as a Loyalist of North Carolina in the American Revolution, supplying important omissions in the copy published in the United States.* Toronto: Reprinted from *The Canadian Magazine,* 1908.

Siebert, Wilbur Henry (ed.). *Loyalists in East Florida 1774 to 1785: The Most Important Documents Pertaining Thereto Edited With An Accompanying Narrative.* 2 vols. Deland, Fla: Florida State Historical Society, 1929.

South Carolina Gazette. Charleston, N. C., 1769, 1775.

Stevens, Benjamin Franklin (ed.). *The Campaign in Virginia 1781. An exact Reprint of Six rare Pamphlets on the Clinton-Cornwallis Controversy with very numerous important Unpublished Manuscript Notes By Sir Henry Clinton K.B. And the Omitted and hitherto Unpublished portions of the Letters in their Appendixes added from the Original Manuscripts.* 2 vols. London: [n.p.], 1888.

Wynne, Thomas H. (ed.). *The Narrative of Colonel David Fanning, (A Tory in the Revolutionary War with Great Britain;) Giving an Account of his Adventures in North Carolina, From 1775 to 1783, As Written by Himself, with an Introduction and Explanatory Notes,* with an introduction by John H. Wheeler. Richmond, Va.: private [Historical Documents Relating to the Old North State No. 1], 1861.

Secondary Sources

General Histories and References

Alden, John Richard. *The South in the Revolution, 1776–1789.* Baton Rouge, La.: Louisiana State University Press, 1957.

Ashe, Samuel A'Court. *History of North Carolina.* 2 vols. Greensboro, N. C.: Charles L. Van Noppen, 1908–25.

Ashe, Samuel A'Court, *et al.* (eds.). *Biographical History of North Carolina From Colonial Times to the Present.* 8 vols. Greensboro, N. C.: Charles L. Van Noppen, 1905–17.

Boatner, Mark M., II. *Landmarks of the American Revolution.* Harrisburg, Pa.: Stackpole Books, 1973.

Britannica Atlas. Chicago: Encyclopaedia Britannica, Inc., 1969.

Calhoon, Robert McCluer. *The Loyalists in Revolutionary America, 1760–1781.* New York: Harcourt, Brace, Jovanovich, 1973.

Cheney, John L., Jr. (ed.). *North Carolina Government, 1584–1974: A Narrative and Statistical History.* Raleigh, N. C.: North Carolina Department of the Secretary of State, 1975.

Gwathmey, John H. *Historical Register of Virginians in the Revolution, Soldiers-Sailors-Marines 1775–1783.* Richmond: Dietz Press, 1938.

Hannay, James. *History of New Brunswick.* 2 vols. St. John, N. B.: John A. Bowes, 1909.

Johnson, Allen, and Dumas Malone (eds.). *Dictionary of American Biography.* 21 vols. New York: Charles Scribner's Sons, 1928–37.

McCready, Edward. *The History of South Carolina in the Revolution, 1775–1780.* New York: Macmillan Co., 1901.

Nelson, William H. *The American Tory.* London: Oxford University Press, 1961.

Peckham, Howard H. (ed.). *The Toll of Independence: Engagements and Battle Casualties of the American Revolution.* Chicago: University of Chicago Press, 1974.

Powell, William S. *The North Carolina Gazetteer.* Chapel Hill, N. C.: University of North Carolina Press, 1968.

Sabine, Lorenzo. *Biographical Sketches of Loyalists of the American Revolution With an Historical Essay.* 2 vols. Port Washington, N. Y.: Kennikat Press [reissue of 1864 edition], 1966.

Smith, Paul H. *Loyalists and Redcoats: A Study in British Revolutionary Policy.* Chapel Hill, N. C.: University of North Carolina Press, 1964.

Stephen, Leslie, and Sidney Lee (eds.). *The Dictionary of National Biography.* 22 vols. London: Oxford University Press, 1917.

Wallace, W. Stewart (ed.). *The Macmillan Dictionary of Canadian Biography* (3rd ed.). London and Toronto: Macmillan Co., 1963.

Ward, Christopher. *The War of the Revolution.* 2 vols. New York: MacMillan, 1952.

Special Studies and Articles

Barnwell, Robert Woodward, Jr. "Loyalism in South Carolina, 1765–1785." Unpublished Ph.D. dissertation, Duke University, 1941.

Howe, Jonas, "Colonel David Fanning: The Career of a Carolina Loyalist of the

Caruthers, Eli Washington. *Revolutionary Incidents: And Sketches of Character Chiefly in the 'Old North State.'* Philadelphia: Hayes and Zell, 1854.

Coleman, Kenneth. *The American Revolution in Georgia, 1763–1789.* Athens, Ga.: University of Georgia Press, 1958.

DeMond, Robert O. *The Loyalists in North Carolina During the Revolution.* Durham, N. C.: Duke University Press, 1940.

Draper, Lyman C. *King's Mountain and Its Heroes: History of the Battle of King's Mountain, October 7th 1780, and the Events which Led to It.* Spartanburg, S. C.: The Reprint Co. [reprint of 1881 edition], 1967.

Drayton, John. *Memoirs of the American Revolution, From Its Commencement to the year 1776, Inclusive: As Relating to the State of South Carolina.* 2 vols. Charleston, S. C.: A. E. Miller, 1821.

"The Family of Joseph Hinds of Guilford and Randolph Counties," *North Randolph Historical Society Quarterly,* VI (Winter, 1972).

Gregg, Alexander, *History of the Old Cheraws.* New York: Richardson and Co., 1867.

Harrell, Isaac S. "North Carolina Loyalists," *North Carolina Historical Review*, III (October, 1926), 575–90.

Howe, Jonas, "Colonel David Fanning: The Career of a Carolina Loyalist of the American Revolution." Unpublished article, Archives of the New Brunswick Museum, St. John, N. B., 1890.

Landrum, J. B. O. *Colonial and Revolutionary History of Upper South Carolina.* Spartanburg, S. C.: The Reprint Co. [reprint of 1897 edition], 1959.

Medley, Mary L. *History of Anson County, North Carolina, 1750–1976.* Wadesboro, N. C.: Anson County Historical Society, 1976.

Newlin, Algie I. *The Battle of Lindley's Mill.* Burlington, N. C.: Alamance Historical Association, 1975.

Olson, Gary. "Loyalists and the American Revolution: Thomas Brown and the South Carolina Backcountry, 1775–1776," *South Carolina Historical Magazine*, LXVIII (October, 1967).

Phifer, Edward W., Jr. *Burke: The History of a North Carolina County, 1777–1920, With a Glimpse Beyond.* Morganton, N. C.: private, 1977.

Ramsay, David. *Ramsay's History of South Carolina from Its First Settlement in 1670 to the Year 1808.* 2 vols. Newberry, N. C.: W. J. Duffie, 1858.

Rankin, Hugh F. *Francis Marion: The Swamp Fox.* New York: Thomas Y. Crowell Co., 1973.

———. *The North Carolina Continentals.* Chapel Hill, N. C.: University of North Carolina Press, 1971.

"Thomas Blair, A Tory Captain," *The North Carolina Genealogical Society Journal*, III (August, 1977), 165.

Troxler, Carole Watterson. *The Loyalist Experience in North Carolina.* Raleigh, N. C.: Division of Archives and History, 1976.

———. "The Migration of Carolina and Georgia Loyalists to Nova Scotia and New Brunswick." Unpublished Ph.D. dissertation, University of North Carolina at Chapel Hill, 1974.

———. "'To git out of a Troublesome Neighborhood': David Fanning in New Brunswick." *North Carolina Historical Review*, LVI (October, 1979).

Waring, Alice N. *The Fighting Elder: Andrew Pickens, 1739–1817.* Columbia, S. C.: University of South Carolina Press, 1962.

Watterson, John S., III. "The Ordeal of Thomas Burke," *North Carolina Historical Review*, XLVIII (April, 1971).

Wilson, Isaiah W. *A Geography and History of the County of Digby, Nova Scotia.* Belleville, Ont.: Mika Studio [reprint of 1900 edition], 1972.

Wright, Esther Clark. *The Loyalists of New Brunswick.* Moncton, N. B.: Moncton Publishing Co., 1955.

Wyche, Mary Clayton. "The Tory War in North Carolina." Unpublished Master's thesis, University of North Carolina at Chapel Hill, 1941.

[141]a GEORGE BAYLOR (d. 1784) of Virginia was a Continental lieutenant colonel and aide-de-camp to General Washington. By January, 1777 he was promoted to colonel and took command of the Third Continental Dragoons. His unit was surprised and destroyed at Old Tappen, New Jersey on September 28, 1778, in a night raid planned by Lord Cornwallis. Baylor was wounded and taken prisoner in the action. By 1782 he was commanding the First Continental Dragoons in South Carolina with General Greene and directed American cavalry operations around Charleston. John H. Gwathmey, *Historical Register of Virginians in the Revolution, Soldiers - Sailors - Marines 1775–1783* (Richmond: Dietz Press, 1938), p. 49. Christopher Ward, *The War of the Revolution* (New York: MacMillan, 1952), pp. 616, 698, 701, 841.

Index